Prairie Homestead to Wall Street

A History of the Jones Family and
Metropolitan Financial Corporation

By the same author

THE DAY OF THE BONANZA

THE CHALLENGE OF THE PRAIRIE

BEYOND THE FURROW

TOMORROW'S HARVEST

KOOCHICHING

PLOW SHARES TO PRINTOUTS

TAMING THE WILDERNESS

HISTORY OF U.S. AGRICULTURE
(a.k.a. Legacy of the Land)

CREATING ABUNDANCE

E.M. YOUNG: PRAIRIE PIONEER

A CENTURY IN THE PARK

Prairie Homestead to Wall Street

A History of the Jones Family and
Metropolitan Financial Corporation

HIRAM M. DRACHE
Concordia College
Moorhead, Minnesota

HOBAR PUBLICATIONS
A Division of Finney Company
www.finney-hobar.com

ISBN: 978-0-913163-44-3

Images from the Jones family collection.

Designed by Angela Wix
Edited by Lindsey Cunneen

Hobar Publications
An Imprint of Finney Company
8075 215th Street West
Lakeville, Minnesota 55044
www.finney-hobar.com

1 3 5 7 9 10 8 6 4 2
Printed in the United States of America

~ Dedication ~

To the memory of my grandfather Martin, my father Maurice,
and my brother Morrie, who devoted their careers to Metropolitan
and their lives to serving society, always guided
by the highest ethical standards.

To my dear wife Eunice,
my silent partner, who helped me overcome my human
frailties and guided me to heights beyond my greatest expectations.

To the many loyal individuals who became part of the
Metropolitan family, a company known for its friendly
atmosphere, where everyone's daily work was a joy.

–Norman M. Jones

~ About the Cover ~

The log cabin as it is preserved today was built in the 1860s and is located on forty acres in section nineteen of township eleven (Freeman) Badax County, Wisconsin. The land was purchased from the government at a public land sale on June 1, 1860, by Christen Simonson, father of Mary Ann, who became Henry Jones' wife. The cabin and other buildings were erected soon after. In March 1864, Henry Jones purchased twenty acres of that land with the cabin for $100. The sturdy log structure was beautifully restored by John and Anne Tedeschi, who have owned it since 1969. This picture was taken in 2001.

The second structure is the home of the New York Stock Exchange on Wall Street. On May 17, 1792, the original members of what became the Exchange met under a buttonwood tree on Wall Street not far from the site of the present building. The new classical-revival style building on Broad Street was opened in 1903. It has been enlarged several times since, but the columned façade remains as a recognizable symbol of Wall Street and the Exchange.

The background is from a reproduction of a painting that was done in 1923 and accompanies the certificate given to every company that becomes a member of the Exchange.

~ About the Author ~

After serving in the Air Force in World War II, Hiram Drache earned degrees at Gustavus Adolphus College, the University of Minnesota, and the University of North Dakota. At the same time he worked in several businesses and taught high school between his college years. He purchased his first farm in 1950 and was involved in farming until 1981, when he sold the family farm and began to lease out the others. He has taught at Concordia College since 1952, and since 1991 has been Historian-in-Residence. This is his twelfth book. In addition, he has contributed to eight others and has written more than fifty articles chiefly on contemporary agriculture and/or agricultural history.

Foreword

When you read a book written by Hiram Drache, you always learn a good deal about economic history, the values of rural America, and changing demographics. You expect and find supporting data and anecdotes for each and every one of Drache's historical observations and claims.

You will find all of this in Drache's history of Metropolitan Financial. But this book is about much, much more than trends and data; it's about the flesh and blood leadership of a talented family and the company they established, preserved, grew, and re-created. There are many themes here but the ones most impressive to me are these four: finance, family, friends, and faith.

Finance provides the framework for this remarkable story. From a company with assets of $25,000 in 1926 to an industry leader with assets in excess of $8 billion in 1994, Metropolitan Financial created history. While some thrift institutions remained small and were forced to invest in marginal mortgages, Metro expanded aggressively and invested conservatively. When the savings and loan crisis jeopardized the savings and investments of millions of people in the eighties, Metropolitan's solid asset base, prudent lending practices, efficient management, and entrepreneurial leadership provided a platform for growth. And grow it did to the benefit of savers, lenders, and investors. The stockholder who invested $1,000 at the first public offering in 1983 would have realized a value of $12,653 in 1994, an annualized return of 30 percent. And thousands of Midwestern people shared in the fruits of this incredible financial miracle.

Family is a second unifying theme in this book. You would correctly think of "family" in the literal sense as the family tree branching from Martin to Maurice, from Maurice to Norman, and then from Norman to Morrie and Mark. It was family working together—often making sacrifices in the early going for the sake of the family's future well-being. There was also family mentoring from father to son and brother to brother.

I also think of family in the figurative sense, that is, the family atmosphere of the company. Employees talked about this consistently. So too did people in the communities in which Metro was located. I think of the family values cultivated by the company whether one refers to the value of thrift and savings as taught through the Johnny Appleseed clubs for children, or the value of hospitality as practiced through the Metro Clubs in a variety of ways, or the value of community exhibited by employees and the banks through their involvement in community projects, or the value of charity as seen in the company's contributions to a variety of good causes, or the values of honesty and trustworthiness that were at the core of the company's operating credo.

Friends come into the story time and again. There were the friends Norman often sought out for counsel before making key decisions, the talented and trustworthy friends who became members of the board of the public company, and friends who were key employees of the company. And while not every key employee was a personal friend coming in, most became friends in response to Norman's outgoing, friendly, and sincere attitude. The significant role of friends in this company story stands in sharp contrast to some contemporary corporate models that focus so heavily on objectivity and results that personal relationships become extraneous to the enterprise.

You cannot read this book without commenting on the role of faith in the lives of Norman and Eunice Jones. This book describes the many forms of public and corporate recognition that have come to Norman, all of it justly deserved. But Norman's style is self-effacing and humble—he has always known that he is a steward of what has come to him from God, that what counts is not how much you "get" by way of honor or influence or wealth, but on how you lead and how you serve and how you share. While Eunice has been a silent but not insignificant partner in the corporate equation, she has been a full partner in the faith equation. Both she and Norman can "give reason for the hope that is in them." Their gracious acts of personal support, their generous acts of stewardship, and their wise acts of leadership all testify to that hope and serve as model and inspiration for others.

Paul J. Dovre
President Emeritus
Concordia College

Preface

Residents of the upper Midwest who enjoy and appreciate the value of history owe a debt of gratitude to Norman and Eunice Jones for funding research and compilation of data to preserve one segment of this area's history, including accounts of their ancestors in Norway, their life on the American frontier, and the history of a nationally recognized financial company. On January 2, 2007, Norman Jones outlined the story that he thought needed to be written. I quickly realized that this was an opportunity to write about a phase of upper Midwest economy different from what I had been researching and writing since the 1960s. The only difference was that instead of entrepreneurs in agriculture, now it was about financial entrepreneurs.

Henry Jones, the first of the four generations in this story, worked as a lumberjack immediately after arriving from Norway. In 1861 he enlisted in the Union Army and was wounded in his first battle. He received a medical discharge and went to Wisconsin to be with the people he had emigrated with from Norway. While recuperating he married a young woman who was born only twenty miles from his birthplace. He recovered, re-enlisted, and remained in the service until 1866 when he returned to Wisconsin to farm. In 1880 he sold his farm, and he and his family moved to North Dakota.

Martin, the second son of Henry and his wife, Mary Ann, was four at the time of the move. Starting at age ten, Martin worked for other farmers during the summer. As soon as his school days were over, he served as a teamster, transporting grain to elevators on the nearest railroad from inland communities and returning with supplies. At age sixteen he worked at a general store, followed by jobs at: a lumberyard, a grain elevator that he managed, and an implement dealer. He also had invested in a sizeable acreage of land. By his early twenties he became involved in the banking business. Martin Jones was a hard worker, well liked, and obviously very capable. In the late 1890s he met and became a partner in various enterprises with H. H. Berg. He also met Berg's sister, Birgit, whom he married in 1900.

Martin was a cautious entrepreneur who found his niche in banking. He shed all other interests and invested his earnings in banks. He amicably severed his partnership with Berg, who was involved in many enterprises and was a major stockholder in Martin's banks. Both men experienced prosperity in the golden years of agriculture, but that all changed with the sharp drop of agricultural prices in 1920. Berg's tractor venture bankrupted him and nearly did the same to Martin.

Martin became a state bank examiner and Birgit supplemented their income by taking in roomers. In 1926 Martin founded Metropolitan Building and Loan Association where he was joined by his twenty-one-year-old son Maurice. The fledgling thrift was carefully nurtured to a solid start until 1932 when it felt the full impact of the Depression. Father and son nursed the small thrift through the 1930s and 1940s with only one loss year. A side venture as land realtors enabled Martin to recoup his finances and gave Maurice a foundation for his. This venture had no bearing on Metropolitan, which became the second largest thrift in the community. Maurice grew in stature in the community, in the thrift industry in North Dakota, and then nationally.

In 1952 twenty-two-year-old Norman Jones, fresh out of military service and undecided about his future, was subtly encouraged to join his father and grandfather in the tiny institution of six employees. Norm had a speech and reading impediment which, with the aid of his parents and his wife, Eunice, he overcame to the extent that it was rarely detected by coworkers or the many audiences that he addressed. Norm was an entrepreneur blessed with a powerful memory, tremendous energy and enthusiasm, and a kind personality. He worked at every level in the business and grew personally as he expanded Metropolitan. He was called an aggressive conservative when it came to running the business, but he was such a student of the industry that he was able to detect trends and use them to Metropolitan's advantage.

Metropolitan became a leader in the industry, and Norm soon was recognized throughout North Dakota, then the Midwest, and finally, nationally for his contribution and guidance. He served on five national boards. Metropolitan became the first company in North Dakota to be listed on the New York Stock Exchange. North Dakotans traditionally were not stock buyers, but their faith in the Jones family and Metropolitan led them to purchase Metro stock, which resulted in more of them becoming wealthy (even millionaires) than from investing in any other company. Douglas Burgum, who was the prime mover in the success of Great Plains Software, now a subsidiary of Microsoft, commented that Metro's success certainly made it easier for his company to sell stock, but he was of the opinion that Metro had a larger number of local investors.

Henry Jones spent forty years of his life with a bullet in his leg received while serving his adopted country in the Civil War. Henry's determination established a legacy that continued with his son, Martin, and grandson, Maurice. Today his great-grandson, Norman, and Norman's wife, Eunice, are spending the rest of their life supporting worthy causes because they believe "that is the thing to do."

–Hiram M. Drache

Acknowledgments

Writing a book is a delightful experience when you are working with two people like Norm and Eunice Jones, who were interested in each chapter of the story of their ancestry and careers. Sometimes they had additional insights, and sometimes I had fresh information. Thanks to both for a delightful time—including the chocolate chip cookies and milk.

Interviewing former employees of Metropolitan was a happy continuation of the time spent with the Joneses because they were all so enthused to talk about the years they had worked *with* the family. Yes, most of them preferred to think of their experience as working with, not for, the family. They were not selected by Norm, because he did not know who I had interviewed until after the fact. The Metro alumni group that meets each year and has maintained a large core of boosters thirteen years after the company was sold is testimony to the esprit de corps that made the company so successful. Norman Jones was an entrepreneur, not an archivist, so he did not have a great collection of data; this made the material gathered from several interviewees especially helpful in getting the little tidbits that add to the story. Thank you, interviewees.

Once again the facilities and staff of the Ylvisaker Library at Concordia College made coming to work each day a pleasure. The entire staff acts as official greeters. I very much appreciate the cozy office and the amenities that go with it. The numbers 3375 are ingrained in my brain, for whenever the computer did not want to do what I needed done, I called that number and one of the technicians had the answer. When all else failed, I rebooted! Thanks, Cindy, and the computer technicians. I appreciate your help more than you will ever know. I will bring a supply of brownies.

For the twelfth time my mate of over sixty years had to take all the quirks out of my writing. She knows I will never learn to spell even with the help of the computer and always puts the manuscript in top shape. I have told her many times that I will never know which of my "golden words" she removed. In the final call I have to assume the full responsibility for any errors, which I gladly accept.

–Hiram M. Drache

Glossary

ARM	Adjusted Rate Mortgage
ATM	Automated Teller Machine
FDIC	Federal Deposit Insurance Corporation
FHLB	Federal Home Loan Bank
FHLBB	Federal Home Loan Bank Board
FSLIC	Federal Savings and Loan Insurance Corporation
IPO	Initial Public Offering
METRO	Metropolitan Building and Loan Association, and any of its successors or subsidiaries
MFB	Metropolitan Federal Bank
MFC	Metropolitan Financial Corporation
MFMC	Metropolitan Financial Mortgage Corporation
MSC	Metropolitan Service Corporation
NRA	National Recovery Act
NYSE	New York Stock Exchange
S&L	Savings and Loan, S&Ls, Building and Loan, and Thrift are used interchangeably
USSLL	United States Savings and Loan League

Table of Contents

Chapter I

Four Norwegian Immigrants on the Dakota Frontier

The Setting

The extensive frontier of the United States, starting in the seventeenth century, proved to be a magnet to people of other nations but particularly to Europeans who realized that opportunity for advancement in their homeland was limited. By the nineteenth century, news about the Great American Frontier had gained sufficient momentum that many Europeans caught America Fever. Starting in 1825, the percentage of emigrants from Norway in relation to its total population was surpassed only by Ireland of those who left their homeland to come to the United States. The following account deals with two men and their spouses-to-be who experienced roller-coaster journeys to live out the American Dream. All had a positive impact on their communities. A member of the fourth generation of one of those couples was responsible for one of the greatest success stories of North Dakota, which made a significant difference on the lives of hundreds of families in Minnesota and North Dakota into the twentieth-first century.

Henry Jones was born in Laerdal, Sogn, in Norway on August 21, 1838, only twenty miles away as the crow flies from his future bride's home, but light years away as far as communication of those days was concerned. Mary Ann Simonson was born in Luster, Sogn, also in Norway, on May 28, 1848. Both were born into families of cotters, and as they grew up they realized that there was little hope of improving their lot if they remained in Norway. They knew of Norwegians from their community who had gone to America and settled in the area of Viroqua, Wisconsin. In April 1857 Henry

Jones joined 306 others from the parish, most of whom left for America. Mary Ann Simonson's family was also in that group. They went directly to a small settlement of fellow Norwegians in West Prairie near Viroqua, Wisconsin. Henry knew of the Viroqua settlement, but until October 4, 1861, his whereabouts are uncertain because he worked in lumber camps near Lansing, Iowa. At that time he enlisted in the Union Army. On April 6, 1862, Henry was wounded on the first day of the Battle of Shiloh, after which he was discharged and sent back to Wisconsin to convalesce. He received a lifetime pension for his wound and carried the bullet in his leg for the rest of his life. The speculation is that he spent his recovery at the Simonson home, and according to Mary Ann's obituary, the couple got married during that time. Henry re-enlisted April 1, 1863, and was assigned railroad guard duty, which resulted in further combat action. After the war ended, he remained on guard and garrison duty until the end of July 1866.

From 1866 to 1880 Henry and Mary Ann Jones farmed and brought ten children into the world, only five of whom survived. Henry heard about the fertile land in the Red River Valley of Dakota Territory and became caught up in the Great Dakota Boom of 1879-1986. Because of increased settlement, his land in Wisconsin had appreciated in value and he sold his farm at a profit. On October 6, 1880, he left for the Valley. The family and machinery arrived in Richland County, Dakota Territory, on November 1, 1880. Surrounded by other Norwegian settlers, he homesteaded the allotted 160 acres in what became Freeman Township.[1]

Martin Jones

Martin, the third eldest of Henry and Mary Ann's children living in 1880, was born February 20, 1876, and is the focus of the story from this point. When Martin was ten years old, like many farm children of those years, he was hired out to herd cattle for a farmer in Veblen, South Dakota, about forty-five miles from his home. During the buggy ride to his job, he lost his bundle of clothes and straw hat and it is reputed that he worked that summer without a hat or any change of clothes. When the summer was over, he received $10, was returned to Milnor, and walked the final twenty-five miles home.

Henry Jones family homestead was on the southeast quarter, Section 8. Note the location of the school in the lower southwest quarter of Section 9. This was twelve miles northwest of Wyndmere (which appears off the map).

He attended country school, which was just across the road from his home. When not in school, he worked at home or for neighbors, but there is no information as to how much formal schooling he received. In 1892 at age sixteen, Martin worked for Mr. Bishop, a store owner in Veblen located on the Sisseton Reservation. On that job he learned to speak some Dakota Sioux. It is uncertain how long he remained there, but from 1896 to 1898 he worked for Mr. Bishop again, this time hauling grain to the elevator on the rail line at Old Wyndmere or to Lidgerwood and DeLamere. He used wagons or sleds depending on the condition of the trails. He returned to Veblen with groceries and other freight. The round trip to and from Wyndmere was sixty miles and took from four to six

HOMESTEAD PROOF.—TESTIMONY OF CLAIMANT.

Henry Jones being called as a witness in his own behalf in support of homestead entry No. _7694_, for _S E ¼ of Sec 8. Town 134" of Range 52"_ testifies as follows:

Ques. 1.—What is your name—written in full and correctly spelled—your age, and post-office address?

Ans. _Henry Jones. I am 43 Years old. My post office is Owego Ransom Co D. S_

Ques. 2.—Are you a native of the United States, or have you been naturalized?

Ans. _I am a soldier and have taken my second papers_

Ques. 3.—When was your house built on the land and when did you establish actual residence therein? (Describe said house and other improvements which you have placed on the land, giving total value thereof.)

Ans. _My house was finished on or about February 7th 1881 I established my residence February 8th 1881 I have one log house 15 x 20, half sod and one frame 13 x 23 feet and one cottonwood and 20 acres broken The value of improvements are in my estimate about 300_

Ques. 4.—Of whom does your family consist; and have you and your family resided continuously on the land since first establishing residence thereon? (If unmarried, state the fact.)

Ans. _Of wife and four children; my family has resided continuously on the land_

Ques. 5.—For what period or periods have you been absent from the homestead since making settlement, and for what purpose; and if temporarily absent, did your family reside upon and cultivate the land during such absence?

Ans. _I have been working out in order to support myself and family and not been absent on more than about one week at the time, and my family has resided there during such absence_

Ques. 6.—How much of the land have you cultivated and for how many seasons have you raised crops thereon?

Ans. _I have 20 acres broke; no crop raised yet_

Ques. 7.—Are there any indications of coal, saline, or minerals of any kind on the land? (If so, describe what they are, and state whether the land is more valuable for agricultural than for mineral purposes.)

Ans. _No_

Ques. 8.—Have you ever made any other homestead entry? (If so, describe the same.)

Ans. _Never_

Ques. 9.—Have you sold, conveyed, or mortgaged any portion of the land; and if so, to whom and for what purpose?

Ans. _No, I have not_

Henry Jones

I HEREBY CERTIFY that the foregoing testimony was read to the claimant before being subscribed, and was sworn to before me this _15th_ day of _February_, 188_2_.

Horace Austin
Register

NOTE.—If naturalized, the claimant must file a certified copy of his certificate of naturalization. In a commuted homestead a foreign-born claimant, if not naturalized, must file a certified copy of his declaration of intention. In making proof, the party must surrender the original duplicate receipt, or file affidavit of its loss.

(SEE NOTE ON FOURTH PAGE.)

1882. Henry Jones' description of his homestead on the homestead proof

Homestead proof filed after Henry Jones had established his 160-acre farm and fulfilled the basic requirements of the Homestead Act.

In 1899 Mary Ann Jones purchased the west half of the east half (160 acres) of Section 32 Helendale Township in Cass County.

days, a task that tested the slender five-foot, nine-inch young man. In the winter he often walked beside the sled to keep from freezing. Martin was twenty-one when his father died.

After arriving in North Dakota, Mary Ann gave birth to six more children, making a total of sixteen. Helena in 1883; John in 1885, who died; Anna Marie in 1887; August in 1889; Christine in 1891; and another John in 1894. On August 1, 1897, Henry died, leaving his forty-nine-year-old widow, Mary Ann, with five children ages three to fourteen still at home. She had the advantage of living on a debt-free farm even though it was not the best piece of land, and she received her husband's $8 monthly pension for her remaining years. On June 29, 1899, Mary Ann used the Soldier's

Widow's Rights and paid an $18 filing fee to secure another 160-acre farm about seven miles from the original farm. So she was by no means destitute. She remained on that property until about 1907 when she moved to a new home in Wyndmere where she resided until her death in 1923 at age seventy-five. In 1921 she had selected a lot in Elk Creek Cemetery south of Wyndmere and had Henry's remains and those of an infant son removed from Freeman Cemetery near their homestead to Elk Creek. It was then that the bullet that had wounded Henry was discovered, which explained his lifelong pain in that leg.[2]

Halgrim Halvorson Berg

Halgrim (hereafter H.H., which he preferred) was born May 17, 1870, at Gøl, Hallingdal, in Norway. He was the eldest son of a farmer who had a sizeable tract of forest land and a small acreage of tillable land; this gave them an advantage over the farmers who had only farm land. H.H. had an entrepreneurial bent, and when he turned nineteen in 1889, he realized that his father was only fifty-one and not ready to retire. H.H. knew that off-farm opportunities were limited in Norway, so he decided to go to America. He traveled directly to his maternal uncle, Nels Brekke, who farmed near Kindred, North Dakota. H.H. spent the first year with the Brekkes working as a hired man. Then he worked on other farms, including a bonanza. In 1895 he established a lumberyard at DeLamere. It is possible that this may have been when H.H. first met Martin Jones, who worked there. H.H. came from one of the largest families in Norway—one relative was a businessman well-known throughout the country—but his parents' holdings consisted only of the property listed above.

Birgit Halvorsdatter Berg

On March 2, 1877, H.H.'s sister, Birgit, was born. In April 1896, after eight years of elementary education, she entered nursing school for training as a midwife at a maternity hospital in Oslo. The 100-mile trip from her home was accomplished by means of a horse-drawn cart, a riverboat, and a train. After graduating from that one-year course in April 1897, she left Norway and followed her brother, H.H., to Kindred, North Dakota. On July 27, 1897, she arrived at the

The farm home of Birgit Berg Jones (Mrs. Martin) in Gol, Hollingdal, Norway. The house is left center with the large chimney.

home of her uncle, Nels Brekke, where she lived for several weeks while searching for work. She was employed by Dr. Fjelde at nearby Abercrombie, North Dakota, where she rode a bicycle to call on sick patients or maternity cases. In 1897 her brother opened a business in Wyndmere, and in 1899 he called Birgit to keep house for him and to continue her nursing in the village.

In the meantime, Martin Jones continued his freighting work as well as working for the lumberyards and elevators, first at DeLamere and then at Wyndmere. At the latter he earned the respectable salary of $65 a month at the Woodworth Elevator and then was employed by H.H. at the Berg Supply House. It is then that he met Birgit Berg, whom he married November 13, 1900. The couple built a substantial house in Wyndmere immediately after their marriage and had three sons: Harold, born in 1901, and twins Maurice H. and Norman B., born May 23, 1905.

Birgit and Martin Jones at Wyndmere, 1900. Possibly their wedding picture.

Ole A. Olson, who was a close business associate of Birgit's brother, knew her from the time she came to Wyndmere in 1899. In 1954 Olson wrote:

> Birgit was an outstanding person, a good cook, and an immaculate housekeeper. She raised her children through sickness and guided them properly so as to make them good citizens and successful businessmen. She saw to it that they all got a good education and had a great deal to do about handling family finances with the result that something of value was left to sustain them in their declining years.

In an undated letter to relatives in Norway, Birgit described her feelings about living on the frontier:

> I would like to express my opinion of what I thought of the North Dakota prairies. I was, naturally, lonesome for the beautiful country I left in Norway, but at the time I left it wasn't easy for farmers in the Gol hills to prosper. . . . The farm land was on the shelves of the hills and amongst the rocks. My father, however, prospered better that most because he owned a large amount of forest and had

Main Street, Wyndmere, c.a. 1906.

considerable grazing land. But actually, being of a thrifty nature, I could see the possibilities of the wonderful rich, black soil in the Red River Valley, and it looked good to me—especially the acres after acres, and I really did not have any strong desire to go back to Norway to live.

Birgit's desire for her sons to become educated is exemplified in a news item in the January 6, 1916, *DeLamere Mistletoe*: "Mrs. Martin Jones and son Harold went to Fergus Falls to make arrangements for Harold to attend high school there." Fergus Falls was fifty-five miles from DeLamere on the Northern Pacific route. Wahpeton was only thirty-six miles away, but in either case Harold would need board and room. It is quite likely Fergus Falls was chosen because the parents of Mrs. H.H. (Emma) lived there. Later, sons Maurice and Norman also went to Fergus Falls. This entailed an added expense but, fortunately, the railroad connection was good.

Martin and H.H. owned much of the land adjacent to the junction of the Soo Line and the Northern Pacific, which was temporarily called East Wyndmere in deference to Old Wyndmere. Wyndmere was on the Northern Pacific line and Mosselle was located south of the junction on the Soo Line. So both towns moved

First National Bank, Wyndmere, 1915. Left to right, Norman B. Jones, Ole A. Olson, Maurice Jones.

to the junction of the railroads and became Wyndmere. The first news of the merger of the two settlements appeared July 21, 1899, when the *Richland County Gazette* reported that the "New Town" at the crossing was the chief topic around Mosselle and Wyndmere. By October H.H. had already put up a new building at the crossing and was prepared to "embark on business there more heavily than ever." The *Gazette* later stated, "The town of Mosselle is growing slowly less. M.L. Hillard's residence is the second that has gone, left today for Wyndmere drawn by forty-eight horses." But it was not until 1902 that the residents of those settlements agreed to merge at the junction and call the new location Wyndmere. Martin reputedly was the last elevator manager to purchase wheat at Old Wyndmere and the first to buy grain at Wyndmere.[3]

Emma Marie Harris

Emma was born January 27, 1878, in Lansing, Iowa, to Martin Knudson Harris and Andrea Evenson Harris. In 1882 her parents moved to Silver Prairie in Richland County and nothing more is known about her until she married H.H. Berg in May 1901.[4]

Real Estate Ventures

The frontier attracted many people because it offered great opportunity for gain. Any citizen or a person who had filed papers to become a citizen, female or male, who was twenty-one years old or the head of a family was eligible to secure 160 acres under the Homestead Act. Many were interested in farming while others came to secure land in hopes of finding a cash buyer for the land and then moving on to other ventures. The risk was great but many were willing to pay the price for the opportunity. It is quite certain that Martin did not bring any money with him. H.H. may have, but this is pure speculation. At this period the national per capita annual income was about $300, and farm laborers earned an average of one dollar per day plus board and room. The great mystery is, even if they had saved half of their earnings, how did they accumulate sufficient funds to purchase land used later to start up their business ventures?

In a search of the Ledger of Original Entries for Richland County, where Wyndmere is located, 133 entries were found that indicated that Martin had purchased 640 acres of land in addition to thirty-seven lots in East Wyndmere between 1895 and 1902, and by 1909 he had sold 320 acres and twenty-six lots. Newspaper accounts covering the eastern portion of the county, which had more developed farms by then than in the Wyndmere area, reveal that 4,172 acres of virgin land in twenty-six parcels sold for an average $8.79 an acre.

Population increased rapidly in the following decades causing the average price to increase from $18 per acre in 1900 to $40 by 1910 and to $80 by 1920. Those years included the Golden Age of Agriculture, 1905-1919, a time during which farmers nationwide enjoyed unprecedented prosperity.

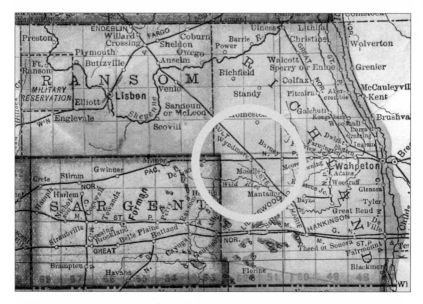

A 1910 map showing only the railroad lines. Note the location of Wyndmere on the Northern Pacific line and Moselle on the Saute Ste. Marie (Soo) line.

Martin was on the ground floor in the merging of Mosselle and Old Wyndmere into the railroad junction community of East Wyndmere. He paid farmland prices for the land which he then converted into town lots. His original cost for an average size lot was $2.89, and, according to the Ledger of Original Entries, average sale price of a lot was more than $100. Based on that information, it is the opinion of this writer that real estate was the basis of the bulk of his early funds. Martin was skillful in leveraging money, but that does not answer where he got the initial funds to purchase the land.[5]

Adventures in Retailing

The Wyndmere Enterprise reported that the Wyndmere Lumber Company offered a complete line of building materials. This firm was co-owned by H.H., Martin, and a Mr. Rolfshus, but managed by Martin and Rolfshus. The lumberyard also had a sawmill, which operated daily to handle timber that settlers brought in to be sawed to their specifications. At the same time Martin also ran a machinery dealership next to the lumberyard. Except for liquidating his real estate holdings, this was Martin's final adventure in retailing, for after 1908 he attended strictly to banking. H.H., on the other hand, was an investor in each of the banking operations and relied on Martin's expertise in management.

On April 10, 1913, the Milnor paper reported that H.H. had received a train-car of six Ford automobiles to be put on display at the CMC store. This was the first indication of his involvement in the automobile business. Sales increased rapidly in 1914 and in 1915 he sold seventy-five cars. On March 2, 1916, it was announced that in the previous three and a half months, he had received seven carloads at the Milnor agency totaling thirty-five cars. Martin was not involved in the automobile business, nor the tractor business started by H.H. in 1915, other than through financing, but this led to a major turn of events for him in 1919.[6]

Banking on the Frontier—Wyndmere

In 1900 James McGann, the Northern Pacific agent in Wyndmere, established the Bank of Wyndmere. In 1901 he sold his interest to E. L. Haney, who later sold his shares to Martin Jones, who became the cashier and held that position until 1908. H.H. also purchased stock in the reorganized First National Bank of Wyndmere in 1904, but in 1906 he left town for other ventures. However, he was satisfied with his other Wyndmere businesses managed by Martin because they were functioning well. In 1908 Martin sold his interest in the Bank of Wyndmere and moved to Lisbon. H.H. retained his stock in the First National Bank of Wyndmere, but did not play a major role there until January 12, 1915, when he was elected president. He attempted to gain control, but when that failed he sold his stock and devoted his efforts to the gas tractor business.[7]

Lisbon

On July 5, 1906, H.H. left Wyndmere to open a bank in Lisbon in temporary quarters formerly occupied by a jewelry store and optician's office. It was called Citizens Bank of Lisbon and boasted $20,000 in capital stock. Again, H.H. relied on his brother-in-law, Martin Jones, to direct the operations. Martin was named president of the Lisbon bank, but because he also was cashier at Wyndmere, he persuaded his older brother, Henry Louis Jones, to move to

Lisbon and handle the duties there. A building was constructed across the street from the Jones Lumber and Implement Company, which Martin still owned.

Lisbon, the county seat of Ransom County, had a population of 1,046. Only five years later, Lisbon had grown to 1,452, but five townships had already lost population, an indication that the area was quite well established and most of the free land had been homesteaded. Lisbon already had two banks and a savings and loan—the State Bank of Lisbon, organized in 1882 with deposits in 1905 of $231,775; the First National Bank, organized in 1883 with deposits of $330,804; and Lisbon Building and Loan Association, with deposits of $56,177. Based on an article in the Lisbon paper, it was obvious that the existing banks were not happy about the new competitor. In July 1905 State Senator Ed Pierce, a Lisbon resident, introduced a bill requesting that no more state banks be authorized unless they had paid-up capital of at least $25,000. The article continued: "Events are demonstrating his wisdom and if he had been sustained there would not be the spectacle of a lot of two-by-four corporations, partly banking with real estate, insurance, and legal paper annexes, now masquerading under the name of banks."

The first ad for the Citizens Bank of Lisbon listed the three officers and stated that it did general banking, paid interest on time deposits, issued drafts for foreign companies, sold steam tickets to all parts of the world, and gave collections prompt attention. It was a poor time to start a bank, for on January 3rd a freight train was stuck in the snow at LaMoure and the tracks remained blocked for most of the month. On January 31st, Lisbon had received no trains for the previous eleven days, and the Southwestern line had received no trains for two weeks. Several communities reported coal shortages. Citizens Bank statement of that date listed total resources of $29,122 after nearly seven months of business.

In May 1907 Citizens Bank announced that it was erecting a 25-x-50-foot two-story brick building with a basement on Fifth and Main Streets "to accommodate their growing business." The August 22nd financial statement gave resources of $36,745, which included the cost of the new building. On the same date State Bank and the First National made far greater gains, proof that they were not easy competitors. But the people at Citizens Bank put up a valiant fight, and on October 3, 1907, the new "solid and substantial building, with interior of hardwood offered cashier Jacobson and his officers as fine quarters as any bank in North Dakota," was opened. The February 14, 1908, financial statement showed that resources had increased to $41,658, which included the new banking house, fixtures, and undivided profits. Sometime in late 1907 Nels Berg, brother of H.H., went to Lisbon as assistant cashier to replace George Jacobson, who won his campaign for county treasurer. In April 1908 Martin Jones sold his interest in the Bank of Wyndmere and moved to Lisbon to become cashier. The paper reported he "had large interests."

For several years throughout the regular spring and fall auction seasons, Martin did extensive clerking at those events. The September 23, 1908, financial statement indicated that the bank was growing, but the competition was still far outpacing Citizens Bank.

No additional news was available on Citizens Bank until March 14, 1910, when L.P. Voisin was listed as president; P.B. Ranes, vice president; and Martin Jones, cashier. The March 29th financial statement showed assets of $80,264. Citizens Bank was still far outpaced by First National and State Bank with assets of $612,837 and $502,695 respectively.

Martin sold his interest in Citizens Bank in 1914. It grew slowly until June 26, 1917, when the cashier, L. J. Bleeker, P.A. Berg (no relation), and others purchased it. They renamed it Ransom County Farmer's Bank and increased the capital stock to $50,000, but to no avail since, like so many other small rural banks, it closed in the mid-1920s.[8]

Milnor

On June 28, 1906, the Comptroller of the Currency, Washington, D.C., announced that it had authorized the establishment of the First National Bank of Milnor which had paid-up capital of $25,000. Martin's only involvement in this bank was as a consultant to H.H. Berg.[9]

Barney

On October 5, 1907, the editor of the *Wyndmere Enterprise* was taken to Barney by Martin Jones in his "10-horsepower machine."

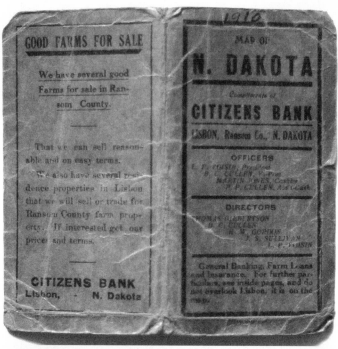

The advertising folder which included the 1910 railroad map previously shown. A farmer presented this to Norman Jones in 1959 when the first Metro branch was dedicated in Wahpeton.

On the way they observed several threshing machines in action and continued to Barney, where they saw a new cement building being erected to house the Bank of Barney in which "the Jones Brothers were largely invested." Just as they were ready to return, the westbound train pulled into town. The editor described the car ride to Wyndmere: "Speeding on the home stretch the machine had the appearance of a comet with a tail extending half a mile to the rear [dust from the road]. Martin disconnected the electrical current and stopped in front of the Wyndmere bank just as the train whistled east of town. We had traveled the seven mile stretch from Barney in exactly twenty minutes—and beat the passenger train into town." With that news the public received the first notice of another bank by the Jones and Berg team.

The Bank of Barney opened October 14, 1907, under the leadership of cashier Henry Louis Jones. He was quoted as saying that "the initial day was quite encouraging and he believed that the people [would] patronize the institution liberally." The bank was capitalized at $10,000. On December 3rd the first financial statement showed total resources of $17,078, which included $2,109 for the banking house and fixtures, $9,216 in loans and discounts, and $2,697 in cash. The board consisted of Henry Jones, cashier; C.E. Harris and J.M. Thiel, directors. At this time Thiel and the Jones Brothers were still involved in the Wyndmere bank. The February report indicated that resources were down from the first report. In October 1908 Cashier Henry Jones was quoted as saying that the Bank of Barney was "enjoying a gradual increase in business and that he was very satisfied with the location." He was confident that Barney had a bright future, as the country was "fast developing."

In December 1908 Henry Jones resigned as cashier at the Bank of Barney and took a position with the Surety Fund Life Company. In March it was announced that he had been elected Wyndmere village assessor. On September 9, 1924, Henry died as a result of a car accident, believed to have been caused by a stroke.

The November 18, 1909, statement showed resources had increased because of new loans and discounts and the amount due from other banks, plus a larger amount in cash. A positive sign was that time deposits totaled $20,234, which is the basis on which a bank operates. During September 1917, sixteen-year-old Harold

Jones, eldest son of Martin and Birgit, was assigned to the Bank of Barney to help cashier Nels Berg during the busy season. Nels managed the bank until it closed in 1933. The population of Barney Township at that time was less than 400.[10]

Gwinner

An ad on March 19, 1908, in *The Gwinner Department*, a supplement of *The Sargent County Teller*, read: "Gwinner State Bank, Gwinner, North Dakota, capital $10,000, surplus $2,000, in 1912 the capital was increased to $30,000." H.H. was president with Martin in the background guiding operations. In February 1919 Harold Jones, Martin's son, accepted a position as assistant cashier in the newly named Farmers State Bank of Gwinner.[11]

DeLamere

Details of the DeLamere State Bank are sketchy but apparently it was founded in 1908 by George Martinson, D.E. Blake, H.H. Berg, and Martin Jones. In September 1914 an agreement was made by Jones, Berg, Blake, and a "Mr. Berg of DeLamere" that made Martin cashier; H.H. president; and Blake was moved to Citizens Bank in Lisbon. Blake had been in DeLamere since the bank had started there and had been a real booster, and it appears he was not happy with the move.

The capital stock at DeLamere was $10,000, but by 1914 the surplus had grown to $15,000. Assets at the time of takeover totaled $113,796 with $87,592 out on loans. The new board consisted of H.H., president; Martin, cashier; G.L.Strobeck, one of the founders, vice president; and George Martinson, assistant cashier. Strobeck had a car agency in Cogswell and later started a bank at Forman. The first ad after reorganization stated, "The fact that the DeLamere State Bank is owned by well-known businessmen and farmers of this community is one of the many reasons why you should have an account at this bank."

Because of the lively economy during these years, there was an active rush for land. By 1915 assets increased over 17 percent to $133,672 with a high ratio of time deposits, a good indication that the bank had patrons of means. The bank strongly encouraged farmers to increase dairying and advertised that it had dedicated

A 2000 highway map of Ranson, Richland, and Sargent Counties showing railroad junction at Wyndmere and communities of Barney, Wyndmere, DeLamere, Milnor, Gwinner, and Lisbon where Martin Jones had direct or silent involvement in community banks.

funds to finance ten silos for farmers who did not have them. "This will improve the financial condition of the community and increase deposits. A silo will double the value of a corn crop."

By 1916 the assets of the bank increased to $141,010, a growth of 24 percent since Martin had taken over as president. This must have been exciting after the experience at Citizens Bank in Lisbon. In 1916 the latest Burrows accounting system was purchased, which eliminated a great deal of writing in recordkeeping.

When the Martin Jones family moved to DeLamere, they lived in an apartment above the Hendrickson General Store, which was just across the street from the bank. The second summer, to escape the heat, they lived in a large, walled tent built on a wooden platform. During a violent thunderstorm the canvas was nearly torn apart and the family members had to hold the ropes to keep loose ends from blowing away. Soon after the family purchased the George Martinson home and built an addition to the house, enlarged the lean-to on the barn and converted it to a two-car garage, and made the barn into an "excellent hen house." The final

19

improvement was pouring cement sidewalks. E.H. Intlehouse, a business associate of H.H. and Martin and a director of the bank, moved into the Hendrickson apartment.

The Golden Years of Agriculture continued to boom, and rural banks prospered. DeLamere State Bank had an excellent year in 1917 and was able to increase its surplus by $5,000. Martin continued to have a good side income from the many auctions that he clerked. By 1917 assets had increased to $230,707, and time deposits were $115,528. By 1918, assets rose to $303,093. The capital stock increased to $20,000 plus $14,444 surplus and undivided profits, while time deposits had risen to $146,468.

The Jones family was set to remain in DeLamere after Martin was elected the secretary/treasurer of the Farmers Livestock Shipping Association. When a bumper crop grew in the area, he spent a week in the harvest fields to help the farmers reap their well-earned rewards. The Jones family was very much involved in the community, and it appeared that they would spend many years at DeLamere. But that was not to be, for H.H. was having problems in his tractor business and needed cash, so the bank was sold. Little did either man realize what the future held for them. The bank progressed until 1920 when it was caught in the collapse of the agricultural economy and then went into a decline until 1930 when it closed, like most other smaller, state-chartered banks.[12]

An Adventure with Tractors

H.H. Berg and Martin Jones had been in business since 1899; they were a great team. H.H. had the ideas and the courage to jump into ventures, always relying on Martin to make the numbers work. This worked fine as long as the economy was in an upswing but, like many entrepreneurs, H.H. could not resist looking for new challenges. If farmers purchased cars as fast as they could be manufactured, surely they would want tractors. In December 1915, after two very successful years with Model T Fords, he took the fatal plunge and contracted for 100 C.O.D. tractors.

On August 17, 1916, H.H. and his family left Milnor for their new home at 1136 North Broadway in Fargo. On their departure from Milnor the editor wrote, "Mr. Berg is a hard-working man and well deserves the success with which he is meeting. There was never anything too difficult for Mr. Berg to accomplish."

A news headline read "H.H. Berg Opens Office in Fargo." The article stated that a temporary office was located in the Metropole Hotel and mailing address was Lock Box 1054. H.H. had opened an office in Fargo to handle the C.O.D. gas tractor. Soon after, he erected a 125-x-25-foot building at 515 Northern Pacific Avenue in which the ground floor was for offices and display space and the basement for repairing. A March 12, 1918, ad in the Fargo paper stated that H.H. Berg, 311 N. P. Avenue, was the distributor for the Allwork Kerosene Tractor. This 5,000-pound tractor was advertised as having fourteen horsepower on the drawbar and twenty-eight on the belt pulley. A June 8, 1918, advertisement described "The Light 'ALLWORK' Tractor, Fully Equipped." This was the last ad for tractors, and there was no other data on that business other than a comment from his son, Elmer, who implied that his father may have even handled a third line. The city directory for 1919 listed H.H. as having Oakland Motor Sales Company. The final newspaper ad for this business appeared December 13, 1919. After that, only his Broadway residence was listed.

By 1919 H.H. and Martin had sold all of their business interests in the rural areas, except for some land that H.H. still owned. The Martin Jones family left DeLamere for Fargo February 25, 1919, where they purchased a home at 1218-11 Avenue North for $5,500. The house was in Birgit's name with a $1,000 mortgage to North Western Mutual Savings and Loan. The following week they returned to DeLamere where they were honored at a farewell party. The *Mistletoe* editor reported: "It was an enjoyable evening despite the nature of the occasion. . . . The Jones family has been an asset to the community and they will be missed." The article closed stating that Mr. Jones was connected with Mr. H.H. Berg in the auto and tractor business, but he was never listed in the Fargo City Directory as being involved in either business. In retrospect this was an excellent time to sell rural banks, land, and other rural businesses, but for the same reason a poor time to venture into the tractor business.

The C.O.D. tractors were not successful because belt pulleys ran off the flywheel to operate the oil pump, fuel pump, and water pump, a major weakness. A more serious problem was caused by the lack of an air cleaner, which allowed dust and dirt to enter the engine, which quickly led to failure. Elmer Berg added that the banks were not financing tractors, so his father offered financing. The tractors were usually sold in the spring on a contract calling for the first half payment the first fall and the balance the second fall. In addition to the lack of an air cleaner, some models had open gears, which limited their performance and led to early failures. In any case, the farmers returned the tractors as soon as they realized what the problem was and did not fulfill their contracts. From previous research this writer is aware that bankers often were more favorable to financing automobiles than tractors because many bankers, like many farmers, were convinced that tractors would not replace horses for farm work.[13]

What Do We Do Now? H.H. Berg

The tractor business wiped out the fortunes that H.H. and Martin had accumulated up to 1919. Fortunately, both owned their homes. H.H. was forty-nine and Martin forty-three. H.H. was tall and rather husky while Martin was five-feet-nine-inches and wiry. Both were healthy, so what caused them to react so differently to their failure? Both had been entrepreneurs, H.H. the more aggressive and Martin the cautious one. H.H. was very talented and was especially good at selling. Was he so much of an entrepreneur that he could not accept working for others? In 1923 he sent his father in Norway a gift to which his father replied,

> Thank you so much. It is good to know that you care about me, who had never done anything special for you. How often I regret that I allowed you to leave . . . especially when I see the sloppy farming everywhere. What were once grazing land and cultivated fields have been reclaimed by birches and thistles.

Then his father gave the number of cattle on the farm thinking that they had done well. It is the impression of this writer that even though H.H. had fallen on hard times, he would not have been excited by the thought of returning to Norway to farm.

In James Skurdall's history of the H.H. Berg family he wrote that H.H. was never able to recoup. He did many things in an effort to improve his income. He sold nursery stock, was a Watkins dealer, repaired Maytag washing machines, and sold oil in fifty-gallon drums to farmers. Probably the most reliable income came from the roomers that Mrs. Berg had in their home. She was accustomed to serving people, for when they lived in Wyndmere, H.H. often brought people home from the store for meals without much advance notice. After 1920 he worked at anything he could because he felt that was the best way to stay healthy.

Emma Harris Berg died at age sixty on November 1, 1938, in Bismarck where their eldest son, H. Milton, was a successful medical doctor. Little is known about how her death might have changed his attitude, but reputedly H.H. remained in good spirits and was always willing to lend a helping hand to anyone in need.

In 1946 at age seventy-six, H.H. purchased a farm. There is speculation that H. Milton may have provided financial assistance for this transaction. H.H. leased the farm out but dreamt that someday he would actively operate it. Those were good years in agriculture, and based on a letter from Birgit Jones, it apparently yielded a good income. He had great satisfaction in going to the farm to "clean up or fix up," and in his typical style probably overworked, which may have hastened his death at age seventy-nine in 1949.[14]

Martin H. Jones

There is no knowledge of what Martin did directly after February 25, 1919, but on July 1, 1920, he was listed on the State Banking Board's report as one of seven deputy bank examiners for North Dakota. He apparently lost little time refocusing his life's journey. He was listed on the same report for 1923. During these years he observed that while many banks were failing, very few savings and loans were failing. His two decades of banking served him well, for during 1924 while he was examining the books of Gate City Building and Loan Association, he was asked to become their assistant secretary and accepted. The minutes of the Gate City regular monthly meeting on March 18, 1925, recorded that the secretary, W. G. Mahon, had resigned and Martin Jones, who was the assistant secretary, was elected to fill the vacancy. At the same meeting director W.F. Kalka resigned and Martin was elected to fill his vacancy. At the March 5, 1926, meeting the board moved that the secretary's salary from the time he entered his duties with the association should be set at $150 a month. The next motion called for the employment of his son, Maurice Jones, as bookkeeper at a salary of $60 a month.

It is not surprising that as soon as it became known that Martin was enjoying a regular income he was confronted by individuals who had or perceived that they had been wronged by him in previous years. The first summons was served February 13, 1929, when John Hendrickson, of DeLamere, brought suit against him and George Carlson. This involved a note that Martin had signed July 8, 1918, for $1,600 at 6 percent interest. Martin was released as a defendant, but the note was still for $1,500 plus the accrued interest. The case was not settled until January 22, 1931, when Carlson assumed full responsibility and paid $2,408. In 1923 Martin was involved in another case in which he and Birgit were defendants and they were listed as administrators of an incompetent. This involved 320 acres of Cass County land and more than $17,000 cash. There was no record of how that case was concluded.

The Moorhead Lumber Company had a note drawn on April 22, 1922, in the amount of $182 at 8 percent interest and due October 1, 1922, against H.H. Berg, Martin Jones, and William Narum, and signed only by H.H. There was a second note on the same date for $100 at the same terms and date but only against H.H. On September 24, 1927, the case was continued against H.H. only in the amount of $407 plus cost, totalling $419. The papers signed November 18, 1927, indicated that the case was settled for the court costs of $12.

On September 13, 1927, the Cass County sheriff served papers originated by the State Bank of Lisbon against H.H. Berg, William Narum, and Martin Jones relative to a demand note signed in the above order on October 15, 1924, for $281 at 8 percent interest. This matter was temporarily resolved November 9, 1927, when a new note was written to cover the original principle, accumulated interest, and court cost, but signed in a revised order by Jones, Narum, and Berg. On July 28, 1928, the bank brought suit again. Apparently nothing was settled, because on August 31, 1931, the Cass County sheriff served a notice and demand before garnishment to Gunder Olson, president of the Metropolitan Building and Loan Association. Then, on September 3, 1931, the sheriff delivered a summons on Martin Jones and Metropolitan, to Oscar H. Kjorlie, vice president of the association, a notice of garnishment against Martin Jones in the amount of $1,382 plus interest at 7 percent from November 9, 1927. The records of what happened in this case are not available.[15]

∿ ∿ ∿ ∿ ∿

1. James Skurdall, *Henry and Mary Ann Immigrants from Sogn; The Jones Family in America 1857-2001*, (privately printed 2001), pp. 13, 17, 26, 34, 35, 37, hereafter Skurdall-Jones. This is a very detailed history of both families in Norway and the United States.

2. Skurdall-Jones, pp. 46, 51, 56-57, 64; Ole A. Olson, The Martin and Birgit Jones Family: Tributes, Reminiscences, and Reflections (A typed manuscript written by Olson July 12, 1954), p. NA, hereafter O. Olson.

3. Skurdall-Jones, pp. 64, 67; O. Olson; James A. Skurdall, *A Berg Family History; Gol, Hallingdal to Richland County, North Dakota*, (privately printed 2003), pp. 34-35, 37-38, 47, hereafter Skurdall-Berg; *The DeLamere Mistletoe*, January 6, 1916; *Richland County Gazette*, July 21, October 27, December 8, 1899.

4. Skurdall-Berg, p. 35.

5. *Breckenridge Telegram*, June 20, July 11, 1896; Thomas J. Pressly and William H. Scofield, *Farm Real Estate Values in the United States by Counties*, 1850-1959, (Seattle, University of Washington Press, 1965), pp. 7, 33, 37; Richland County, North Dakota, Ledgers of Original Entries, July 16, 1897 to October 4, 1922; *Sargent County Teller* (Milnor) June 27, 1912, February 6, 1913, March 4, August 4, 1915; *The DeLamere Mistletoe*, May 11,1916.

6. *Richland County Gazette*, September, 27, 1901; *The Wyndmere Pioneer*, May 10, 1918; *The Wyndmere Enterprise*, October 1, 8, 1908, April 29, December 2, 1909; Skurdall-Berg, p. 41; *Sargent County Teller*, February 9, 1909, February 8, 1912, April 10, 13, 17, 1913, October 15, 1914, December 16, 1915, February 24, March 2, March 2, August 17, 1916; *The DeLamere Mistletoe*, December 23, 1915, March 1, September 6, 1917.

7. *The Breckenridge Telegram*, January 12, 1895; *The Wyndmere Enterprise*, March 10, 1908, January 1, 14, 1909, March 4, 1915, January 14, 1916; Skurdall-Jones, p. 61; *The Sargent County Teller*, January 14, 1915.

8. *The Lisbon Free Press*, July 27, August 3, 31, 1905, November 15, 1906, January 3, 31, February 14, May 9, 16, July 11, September 5, 26, October 3, 1907, February 27, 1908.

9. *The Sargent County Teller*, September 27, 1906, January 31, November 28, 1907, May 28, 1908, January 26, 1910, February 16, March 16, December 14, 28, 1911, February 8, 1912.

10. *The Wyndmere Enterprise*, October 5, 15, December 10, 1907, March 10, October 15, 1908, January 14, March 18, November 25, 1909; Skurdal-Jones, p. 111; *The DeLamere Mistletoe*, September 6, 1917.

11. *The Sargent County Teller*, March 19, 1908, August 17, December 28, 1911, January 18, 1912;

12. *The DeLamere Mistletoe*, February 27, 1919; *The Sargent County Teller*, September 24, October 1, 1914; *The DeLamere Mistletoe*, July 9, October 22, 1914, May 13, September 16, 23, 1915, August 7, September, 14, 28, November 2, 1916, January 18, June 28, September 6, 1917, March 4, April 11, August 8, 1918, January 16, 1919; Skurdall-Jones p. 61; Skurdall-Berg, p.49.

13. *The Sargent County Teller*, January 13, February 24, July 29, 1916; *The Wyndmere Pioneer,* January 21, 1916, September 6, 1918; *The DeLamere Mistletoe*, August 24, 1916, January 16, February 20, 27, March 6, May 22, 1919; *The Fargo Forum*, March, 12, June 8, 1918, December, 13, 1919; Skurdall-Berg, p. 39; Skurdall-Jones, pp. 49, 61; *Fargo and Moorhead Directory*, (Fargo: Pettibone Directory

Company 1916, 1917, 1919, 1922, 1924), hereafter FMDirectory; Randy Leffingwell, *Classic Farm Tractors: History of the Farm Tractor*, (Motorbooks - International Publishers & Wholesalers), pp. 173-174.

14. Skurdall-Jones, p. 61; interview of Allen Golberg, Pelican Rapids, Minnesota, June 27, 2007, hereafter Golberg interview; Skurdall-Berg, pp. 35-37, 39, 41.

15. Skurdall-Jones, p. 70; Report of the State Banking Board from July 1, 1920, to June 30, 1922, and the Fiscal Year Ending June 30, 1923; Minutes of the Gate City Building and Loan Association, March 5 to May 15, 1925; Ledgers of Cass County Civil Action –Plaintiffs and Defendants, North Dakota Institute of Regional Studies.

Chapter II

Martin H. Jones' New Venture
1926-1952

A Brief History of the Thrift Industry

At the time of our nation's first census, over 90 percent of the population lived on farms. However, as industrial activity became increasingly important, people began to work in urban communities and they needed a place to live. Unfortunately, most of them did not have money to buy or to build a home. In 1831 the workers in the local textile industry in Frankford, Pennsylvania, had come from England and were knowledgeable about the cooperative programs there. They founded the Oxford Provident Building Association, which had a designated, limited life span. People pooled money, then built their homes, and once the homes were paid for, the association was dissolved. A more permanent plan had to be devised that appealed to savers, who had to plan for future borrowing and in the meantime wanted to put savings away.

In 1859 the Pennsylvania Assembly established a new system. It was entirely mutual and more liberal in its return of profits. It was the only plan by which "a working man could become a capitalist and create a source of wealth to supply all reasonable demand."

In 1892 the United States Savings and Loan League (USSLL) was founded to act as a national trade association for its members. In 1894 a precedent-setting incident took place when the Wilson Tariff Act was passed; it proposed a tax of 2 percent on the net income of corporations. The Supreme Court declared, "Nothing herein contained [in the act] shall apply to building and loan associations or companies which make loans only to their stockholders." This was a boon to the thrift industry, and by 1930 it provided about 35 percent of all funds needed for non-farm

27

homes, giving the United States a record 46 percent in home ownership. But the industry was still not well known because 90 percent of the associations had less than $1 million in assets. They could not afford a building, so they were not visible on Main Street. Metropolitan's first office was on the third floor of a bank building.[1]

Changes in the Thrift Industry

The industry was further handicapped because it operated under state charters, and every state had a different set or a total lack of regulations. Because of this, out of 13,975 state banks in 1929, most of the 5,102 banks that failed by 1932 were members of the state banking system. Of the 21,751 member banks in the national bank system, only 846 failed. Depositors became skeptical and withdrew their money and other securities, placing them in safety deposit boxes or hid them in their homes. This decreased the money supply. The second problem was that most thrifts (thrift, building and loan, savings and loan, and S&Ls are used interchangeably) could not afford a full-time secretary, i.e. manager, to run the business. The industry needed to operate more professionally to regain the confidence of the customers and to become politically proactive.

On July 22, 1932, the USSLL realized the first results of its political action when the Federal Home Loan Bank System was signed into law. This act provided funds to most financial institutions. For any association to participate in the Federal Home Loan Bank (FHLB), it had to buy stock equal to 1 percent of the home mortgage loans it had outstanding. To strengthen the entire system, the FHLB required that each association had to provide a thorough financial statement.

To further strengthen the system, on June 13, 1933, Congress passed the Home Owners Loan Act, which permitted granting federal charters to savings and loan associations. This established the procedures as to how member associations were to be operated. Federalization was significant because it standardized operations and helped regain the confidence of the public. Of special importance to the public was the passage of the National Housing Act of January 3, 1934, which insured individual savings accounts of member associations up to $5,000. All federally chartered associations were required to pay ¼ of 1 percent on deposits to the Federal Savings and Loan Insurance Corporation (FSLIC) to insure customer accounts.

By 1935 the worst was over, but by then about 1,500 of the 12,343 associations had gone out of existence. The remaining thrifts were faced with a major setback; by making foreclosures they had accumulated a portfolio heavy in real estate, which had declined in value. Fortunately, the economy improved, real estate increased in value, and the associations regained their liquidity.[2]

The Local Setting

David Danbom, writing in *Going It Alone: Fargo Grapples with the Great Depression*, describes the community in which Martin sought to establish his new venture:

Fargo was the leading retail, wholesale, and service center in North Dakota, and less tangibly, the focus of a disproportionate share of its entrepreneurial energy. Fargo was the biggest success story in a region in which success was not assured, and its success gave it confidence. It was confident it could surmount hard times, even if they originated elsewhere, and it was confident in its continuing growth and bright future. This confidence was not misplaced. . . . Fargo grew while much of the region . . . dealt with contraction. At the end of the Depression its regional economic dominance was greater than at the beginning. Fargo was a winner at the beginning of the Depression and a winner at the end and that fact is an important part of this story.

Danbom's closing sentence referred to Fargo, but it fits the Jones-Metropolitan story well. If Metro had been located in any other town in the state, it probably would not have survived. The following explains why.

The number of farms increased slowly from 1920 to 1930 and then jumped sharply. Because of a massive federal rural rehabilitation program, numbers peaked in 1935, but by 1940 the number of farms dropped quickly to less than the 1920 figure. During the 1930s, rural farm population dropped by 17.5 percent

Martin Jones as state bank examiner, 1922-1924.

and the state's population declined 5.7 percent, but Fargo grew by 13.8 percent.

The agricultural boom and the subsequent euphoria ended in 1919, and starting in 1920 banks began to fail. By 1933 a total of 573 of 898 of the state's banks, or 63.8 percent, were closed. Of those that failed, 479 had loaned out 120 percent of deposits, and the 94 national banks had loans ranging from 47 to 285 percent of deposits. Even farmers who had no loans were affected because their savings accounts were lost in the failed banks. In Fargo, Public Works Administration projects kept the retail trade solvent, and by 1934 Herbert G. Nilles, attorney for Metropolitan Building and Loan and incoming president of the Chamber of Commerce, announced, "We are over the hump, [and] should prepare for increasing prosperity."[3]

Establishing Metropolitan Building and Loan Association

As stated previously, Martin learned from his work as an examiner that savings and loans apparently fared better than banks. As a state bank examiner, Martin had examined the books of Gate City Building and Loan Association, which was established in 1924, and became acquainted with the leadership. His many years of experience paid off. For some unknown reason, Gate City's secretary left, and in March 1925 Martin was engaged for that position. He enjoyed his work with Gate City, which was off to a good start. But, as time passed, because of his strong principles he faced a personal problem. A Mr. Stoddard, one of the directors, was an alcoholic, and Martin let it be known that he would not remain if that individual stayed. When ninety-nine-year-old Ben Holt, a Gate City customer, was interviewed by this writer in 1977, he told how he became involved with Gate City and later with Metropolitan. Holt emphasized that that was why Metropolitan was created: "Martin Jones left Gate City because of Stoddard's drinking."

Martin told his wife, Birgit, that he might like to organize a savings and loan. She replied, "Well, why don't you do it?" He knew how conservative she was, so her spontaneous response gave him the confidence to act. He had strong faith and little to lose, all sectors of the national economy—except agriculture—were doing well, and Fargo's economy was strong, so he went ahead with his dream. His grandson, Norman M. Jones, averred that Martin's strong principles regarding alcohol was the direct cause of his resignation and led to the establishment of Metropolitan.

When Martin moved to Fargo in February 1919, he gave first consideration to the welfare of his sons when he purchased a very small house at 1218 11th Avenue North across the street from North Dakota Agricultural College and the North Dakota Agricultural High School. Son Maurice graduated from the Agricultural High School and then attended the Agricultural College for one year. It was during his high school years that he met Minnie (Min) Dustrud. Min was the seventh of nine children whose father died when she was six. Her widowed mother had left the farm and moved to Fargo so the children could attend high school.

On March 5, 1925, Maurice had completed a year of college and was employed as assistant secretary at Gate City. After his father

The first office of Metropolitan Building and Loan (later renamed Savings and Loan) was located on the third floor of the Fargo National Bank from September 1926 to January 1930.

decided to found Metropolitan, Maurice used his spare time to work on the details of founding the new association while his father sought potential board members and investors. Maurice apparently liked the business and decided not to return to college, and on July 23, 1926, he and Min were married.

When the new firm was founded in September, he became its assistant secretary, a position he held until January 1, 1946, when he became the secretary. Attorney Herbert G. Nilles was named counsel for the new firm, which proved to be the beginning of an association with the Nilles family that continued for the entire history of the company. Martin's eldest son, Harold, suggested Metropolitan Building and Loan as the name for the new enterprise. On September 26, 1926, it received a charter and became the fourth thrift firm in Fargo.

The original board consisted of: John H. Dahl—mayor of Fargo and founder, secretary, and general manager of Northwestern Mutual Fire Insurance Company, and owner of J.H. Dahl Insurance Agency—president; Goodwin J. Hoff, a local insurance agent, vice president. Other directors and investors were: Oscar H. Kjorle, secretary/treasurer of Magill Company, one of the larger grain firms in the area and farm owner; W.E. Black, an immigration agent for the Canadian government who also was a director of Gate City. He later established his own insurance and investment business and also was a director of Western States Mutual Insurance Company; and Martin, "the spark plug and organizer," secretary and manager.

A previous history stated that Martin knew that to get a charter he needed to prove that he could get individuals to pledge to open savings accounts if he would open a building and loan association. It is reputed that with the help of son Maurice, Dahl, and Hoff, Martin "succeeded in beginning a new company with no start-up capital other than the confidence of the people."

The original office location was on the third floor of The Fargo National Bank Building on the northwest corner of Broadway and N.P. Avenue. In addition to direct savings accounts, the chief method of raising money was by selling investment savings accounts in denominations of $5, $10, and $25 drawing 2 percent interest and maturing in ten years. By June 30, 1927, the $25,000 in original assets had grown to $65,283 plus $4,813 in undivided profits and reserves. Six months later assets were $123,679. The first approved loan application was for $2,500 on the residence of Hilma Ringsborg, which was located on Lots one and thirty-seven in McCormack's Addition in Grand Forks. The fledgling enterprise was off to a good start.

Board president John Dahl helped to get Metropolitan established, but in 1928 personal business necessitated that he step down from the leadership role. Martin needed to find another leader with the broad contacts that Dahl had and turned to Gunder Olson of Grafton, who had served as the first sheriff of Walsh County and as a state senator. He moved to Fargo after he became an IRS collector. Because he was so widely known in state political and business circles, he was the obvious choice for president and served Metropolitan well in several positions for the next seventeen years.

The presidency was chiefly a figurehead position, as was true of most of the board positions because the secretary was the manager and working executive. In 1928, in an effort to get a broader representation, the bylaws were amended to increase the board from five to seven. Ben Holt was added to the board at this time and Dahl remained until 1930 when he was succeeded by R.J. Thies, a grain buyer from Durbin. Thies was the first non-Fargo resident to sit on the board, but he had excellent rural connections in a strong agricultural section of Cass County.

The employees in 1928 were: Harold Jones, stenographer, salesperson, and collector; C.B. Paulson, cashier; Mariam Hild and Irene Rasmussen, bookkeepers who both served Metro for many years; Martin, secretary; and Maurice, assistant secretary. The directors were: Holt and Kjorlie, vice presidents; Black, treasurer; and Dahl, president. Under their leadership business continued to grow through 1928, and on January 1, 1929, total assets were $270,968; six months later the figure was $380,602. An ad in the October 5, 1929, *Fargo Forum* read:

> Establish your credit by joining this Association. Many a "live wire" would be a dead end if it were not for connections. Every businessman knows the value and importance of his connections because next to ready money the most valuable thing he can have is credit. Credit is founded as much on a man's personal character and habits as on his possessions or assets. Your membership in this Association brings you in contact with other people who are forging ahead. It gives you a higher standing in the community.

In November, an ad showing "Fargo's 100 Percent List in the Chest Drive"— firms in which everyone donated to the Community Chest Drive—included Metropolitan Building and Loan Association. On January 1, 1930, total assets were $565,237 with undivided profits and reserves of $31,652, which indicated that it was making money. This was a positive sign for the thrift, coming so quickly after the November 1929 Wall Street collapse—an indication that people felt safe putting their money with it. A week later *The Fargo Forum* published a notice of the regular semi-annual dividend of 7 percent on all Class "H" and Class "K" shares and the regular cash dividend on Class "J" investment shares and Class "B" savings shares. The next ad stated, "When you save with a definite purpose in mind—the building or owning your own home—saving is easy. We have always paid 7 percent dividends on monthly savings shares, and 6 percent on fully paid shares."

More space was needed, and between January 8 and 21, 1930, a move was made to a larger office in the Improvement Building at

Metropolitan's second office on Roberts Street and First Avenue North, January 1930 to September 1931.

641 First Avenue North, sometimes referred to as the corner of Roberts Street and First Avenue North. Business activity was not disrupted, for by January 31, 1930, assets had increased to $603,105 and the number of members had surpassed 5,000. This steady growth enabled management to keep funds profitably invested in "good first-mortgage homes." A catchy ad in the Sunday addition of the February 9, 1930, *Forum* read,

> Diversify: That's the Order of the Day—When you invest in the Metropolitan Building and Loan Association you have made a HIGHLY DIVERSIFIED INVESTMENT.—The reason is that ...you are participating in hundreds of selected first-mortgage homes—on [more than 300] North Dakota homes only—but not all in any one city, nor any one class of people.

The thrift industry did well in North Dakota, and in 1930 the members of the state Savings and Loan Association gained 1.5 million dollars in assets. Home ownership rose to 65.3 percent, a healthy gain over the previous years, and the state achieved the highest percentage in the nation in that respect. The thrift industry was aided in January 1931 when Governor George R. Schafer (no relation to Nancy Jones Schafer or Governor Ed Schafer) addressed the legislature about the need to develop a new code to govern the incorporation and operations of the building and loan associations. At the same time he zeroed in on banks that were not properly prepared to finance the raising and feeding of livestock.

Many of the recommendations were enacted by the legislature. But legislation could not stem the downturn in the economy. Savings continued to increase in 1931 but at a slower rate. An ad from the March 5 *Fargo Forum* is the first indication about a softer economy. For the first time they advertised that money deposited by the tenth of the month would draw earnings from the first. The ad continued that savings left with the association would be safeguarded and would be loaned for homebuilding, which meant work for carpenters, masons, electricians, painters, lumbermen, hardware dealers, and allied material dealers, all of which contributed to "a more speedy return of prosperity."

In September 1931 the office was moved to a third location, this time to the first floor of the Universal Building on Fifth Street and Fourth Avenue North. The address was given as the Metropolitan Building. It is during this period that Metropolitan became more aggressive, and either Martin, or more often Maurice, was on the road calling on people throughout the state soliciting funds for savings accounts. They particularly concentrated on school teachers and railroad employees because they made up the largest portion of individuals with a regular income. Maurice's wife, Min, recalled that he crisscrossed the state searching for anyone with a steady income. Norm recalled that many years later he had the satisfaction of hearing many people tell him that "getting started saving money was the greatest thing anyone had ever done for them."

Newspaper ads appealed to specific individuals in which they offered a booklet, "Savings with Safety." The ads pushed the Class "H" Installment Shares, which meant purchasing twenty $50 shares payable for "approximately 132 months." They paid a higher dividend than any other plan. The first four installment payments were applied as the $50 membership fee in the Association and could not be withdrawn if the patron stopped making their monthly deposits prior to fulfilling the contract. After that the remaining principle could be withdrawn on thirty days notice with accrued

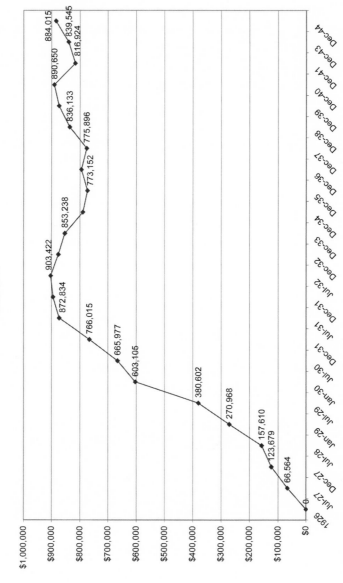

Assets in Thousands of Dollars
1926-1944

Assets in thousands of dollars, 1926-1944. Compare this chart (in thousands of dollars) with the one in chapter four, page 87 (in millions), and the one in chapter six, page 173 (in billions).

interest. From 1930 to 1932, Metro had four individuals on the road selling Class "H" shares; Maurice often was one of them. The campaign was very successful. Assets climbed until November 7, 1931, when they reached $900,626 and undivided profits hit a high of $33,287. On July 1, 1932, assets hit a high of $903,422 and then a decline set in. Little did any one realize how long the recovery process would last.[4]

Building a Firm Foundation, 1932-1952

To cope with the tight money supply and entice savers, advertising tactics changed sharply, as the following ads illustrate: "Rainy Days Do Come. Prepare for Them—$500 can be yours by saving a $1.25 a week for 6.5 years." "Send for our circular 'In a Class By Itself—Building and Loan Shares [the] Only. . . Investment Which Stays at Par.' Special Complimentary Gift to those starting now." Another ad read, "For Thrift Week—January 17 to 23, 1932, mail the coupon with $5 to start a savings or investment account and receive an electric clock free to assist you in beginning 1932 right." The ad tactic that was used for the longest period stated, **"Interest Notice!** Funds deposited at the Metropolitan . . . Association by January 10 will earn interest as from January 1, 1932. Our members know that funds received by the 10th of **Any Month** receive interest from the 1st of same month." A large ad with this notice was run the first of every month for several years.

A sizable ad on January 1, 1933, may have been a bit premature. It read:

> **The Show is Over.** That famous drama, 'The Bulls and the Bears,' that has held the board for the past two years is now closing. Depression is passing, confidence reviving, and most all people have lost interest in the big show. Short cut[s] to riches are always strewn with obstacles and pitfalls. [A brief dissertation on risk followed and then the ad continued.] We, who concentrate on safety and security, never claim to double your money overnight. However, we can over a period of years. We believe that 5 percent dividends with safety are all that any concern should and can pay in times like these.

An ad in the *Fargo Forum* on February 5, 1933, following Metropolitan's Better Business week, indicates that some progress was made in 1932. Ben M. Holt stated that 649 new savings accounts had been made, many with fully paid shares. W.E. Black noted that reserve funds had grown by $7,700, and undivided profits had increased by $3,760, plus they had $19,040 in savings accounts in Fargo banks. Martin added that the association had paid $42,500 in dividends.

Some time prior to January 15, 1933, Metropolitan joined the United States Building and Loan League in addition to being a member of the North Dakota Building and Loan League. In July an ad announced that effective June 15, 1933, the association had joined the Federal Home Loan Bank (FHLB) which, as stated above, provided federal funds to member thrifts for repairing, remodeling, or construction of homes. The purpose of the legislation was to support the thrifts with funds for home builders and thereby provide employment. Fargo received a regional office to work with local associations.

A full page ad on Sunday August 13, 1933, was sponsored by all Fargo financial institutions promoting the National Recovery Act (NRA). But a separate ad sponsored by Metropolitan read,

Make Your Savings Do Their Part to Help NRA Win Back Prosperity. It may be that you cannot directly employ people, raise salaries, shorten working hours, etc., but you CAN MAKE YOUR MONEY DO THAT VERY THING. You can get your dollars into BUILDING AND LOANING activity and thus put them in the front lines of this terrific battle to beat the times. . . . EVERY NAIL YOU'RE SAVING DRIVES INTO THE BUILDING OF SOMEONE'S HOME IS A NAIL SOLIDLY HAMMERED INTO THE COFFIN OF OLD MAN DEPRESSION.

On March 19, 1934, the financial institutions of Fargo-Moorhead announced that they were going to change their opening hour from 9 a.m. to 10 a.m. as a precaution against daytime bank robberies. Experience had shown that most of the robberies took place shortly after opening and in banks that had an early opening hour, especially in cities the size of Fargo-Moorhead. There would be no reduction in the number of employees, or hours of work or wages and salaries paid. Nor would there be any reduction in customer service. The chief impact would be to give more time to the accumulated details, mailing, and posting machine work, and "it should reduce the hazards of holdups."

Assets fell to a low of $773,152 on December 31, 1935, and undivided profits and reserves had declined to $10,745. The high point for real estate owned came in 1937 when that figure reached $160,624, which was 20.7 percent of total assets. This had a negative impact on the returns because there was no income from non-performing real estate.

By 1936 a total of 1,336 associations, which was 11 percent of all the associations nationwide, had 30 percent of all assets of the savings and loans. Of those, 237, including Metropolitan, were state chartered and not insured, but Metro was one of the few that survived. In 1938 Metro's deposits became FSLIC insured. By 1939 about 2,000 of the S&Ls were restricted to the sale of real estate owned and collecting interest and principal on existing mortgage loans. Most of them were not FSLIC insured, and when their assets were sold, they went out of existence. By the early 1940s there were only about two dozen problem cases left.

The national economy started to make a gradual recovery after 1935-1936, but North Dakota was hard hit by drought in 1936 and did not materially regain momentum until the rains came in 1938. In his annual report for 1940 the state bank examiner wrote:

> Taken as a whole, operations for the year have produced a substantial increase in volume, a decidedly improved position in the way of liquidity and a considerable reduction in liabilities other than those to shareholders. Real estate owned, together with real estate sold on contract, represent better than 10 percent of combined assets and constitute one of the major problems of many associations. Earnings for the year, while moderate, were generally satisfactory and adequate to cover reasonable dividend and reserve requirements.

An ad in the *Fargo Forum*, April 12, 1936.

The Metropolitan office in the former Globe Clothing Building, later Straus Clothing, 609 First Avenue North, 1938-1955.

In 1938 Metropolitan moved to the Globe Clothing Building at 609 First Avenue North. All the employees remembered the 14-x-50-foot space with a basement, which was not well suited as an office.

Maurice recapped what it was like at Metropolitan from the peak in late 1931 until the revival:

> From November 30, 1931, to 1943 there was no gain [we] just held our own like most financial institutions did at that time, except those that went broke. Savings and loans, however, had a very good record. Even during this period . . . losses for . . . all savings and loan associations had an unbelievable record with losses less than 1/200 of 1 percent of their assets per year.

The advertising motto for 1943 was "Teach your dollars to have more cents."

The Association was on solid ground, and on January 1, 1946, seventy-year-old Martin yielded his position as secretary to Maurice and assumed the office of president, a position he held until he retired December 31, 1952. In a speech given in the mid-

A *Fargo Forum* ad, July 24, 1938.

A *Fargo Forum* ad, June 9, 1940.

Martin Jones at work during his years as president, 1946-1952.

1960s, Maurice, then a forty-year veteran of the business, probably oversimplified the workings of the thrift industry when he stated that,

the purpose of a savings and loan is to promote thrift and home ownership. It is owned by members and its profits must be shared and distributed mutually among its members prorated according to savings and investment. The operation is simple—receiving money from savers and loaning it out to borrowers for purchasing a home.

Metropolitan was fortunate to have an extremely capable and well-trained leader step in at a time when the potential for growth was probably the best that it had been any time in the past half-century. In 1940 Metropolitan represented 10 percent of the total volume of the seventeen-member North Dakota Building and Loan Associations, and it was located in the largest, fastest growing, and economically the most diversified community in the state. That year Washington Building and Loan, of Fargo, was in liquidation as were associations in Jamestown, Lisbon, and Minot. His father had given Maurice a relatively free hand in the business, so he was well seasoned and not taking over because of his heritage for he had earned his stripes. Maurice was such a likeable, well-versed, and knowledgeable individual that he served as a counselor to many, which proved to be a great asset to the Association. He had the same reputation and respect in the savings and loan industry throughout the region, all of which laid a solid groundwork for later years.

In his speech Maurice stated, "After 1943 we were really on the move. We grew from $900,000 to $2.5 million in 1951, to $7 million in 1954, and to $46 million in 1965. But today the competition is keen." As the economy improved, all savings and loans experienced a steady increase in deposits to the point that some of them wanted to restrict deposits. Income improved as the repossessed real estate was sold. Returning veterans married and the baby boom spurred the economy. At the same time housing starts, which had been at a low for nearly fifteen years, surged.[5]

The Third Generation Enters the Scene

Norman M. Jones was born August 28, 1930. By then his parents had moved from a "tiny 720-square-foot house" on South Fifth Street to North Fifth Street to be closer to Martin and Birgit Jones. Norm commented that the earliest memories he had of his grandparents were after his parents moved to the north side and the two homes were only about six blocks apart. He remembered that his grandfather taught Sunday school for thirty years, and he always picked up his grandchildren because classes were the hour before the church services, which his parents attended. Norm did not recall that his grandfather served on any boards other than as secretary of the Fargo Union Mission (after 1986 better known as the New Life Center) for at least twenty years.

Norm recalled:

We kids had no idea about the company. When I started working I found out how small it really was. Our first home was a tiny house on Fifth Street South, and in 1937 when the folks bought an older two-story house on Fifth Street North, I wondered why we had to rent out rooms. We had four nurses in two rooms, plus cousin Elaine and sister

45

Birgit and Martin Jones on the steps of First Lutheran Church, 1947.

Marlys in a third room, and aunt Ella Rudd in the fourth room upstairs. My parents converted the den into their bedroom on the main floor; my sister Carol and I each had a bedroom in the basement. Mother always used the upstairs bathroom and Dad used the downstairs one. I did not know the answer until after I started working at Metro and realized that the extra income was needed to make the mortgage payments.

Sometime during the late 1930s Martin purchased a home at 1021 Eighth Avenue North, which was near Maurice's family. Birgit continued to have roomers, mostly nurses, to supplement their income. Allen Golberg, who was dating Min Jones' niece Elaine Rudd, recalls that Birgit, who was in her late sixties then, was a fantastic cook and enjoyed hosting family events. Golberg noted that even though the family was very close, he was included as one of them.

Norm had a long bout with pneumonia when he was in the sixth or seventh grade, and in the summers after that his father started taking him along when he traveled to the small towns in the state trying to collect on loans made during the 1930s. Most often the traveling was to places like Cooperstown, Oakes, Valley City, and other small places where Metro had made small commercial real estate loans, which was all the company could offer other than home loans and savings accounts. Many loans in those locations were made to railroad workers and teachers who also made up the majority of the savings account holders during the 1930s. Norm gained some insight into the effort that it took to keep the books balanced at Metro.

It was during these years that he started a lifelong friendship with David Green, who lived only a few houses from the Joneses. Green said, "Norm had a reading problem and he stuttered, plus he was heavier than most so he was not agile in sports, which made him a target for ribbing by some of his classmates. 'Jonesee Jonesee rubber bonesee' was a favorite of some of the nastier classmates." Green continued, "Norm was so positive that it took more than that to discourage him. He was very competitive and wanted to win." At age thirteen Norm had his first experience in leadership when he became a leader in the Eagle Patrol and Green was his assistant leader. Norm felt that Boy Scout Camp was a very positive experience that gave him self confidence.

Norm was fortunate to have very caring parents. Maurice and Norm attended Dale Carnegie courses and convinced Elmer Berg, son of H.H. Berg and cousin of Maurice, to join them. Soon Norm joined Toastmasters International and was "in the same club that Bill Guy attended prior to becoming governor." This gave him confidence to project himself, a trait that strengthened as he realized the progress that he was making. This training, and later encouragement and cooperation from his wife, Eunice, enabled him to become a very effective and forceful speaker. About 1983 Norm's mother, Min, told this writer that she credited much of Norm's

47

success to Eunice because "she overlooked his impediments and saw the drive he had to overcome them." Norm's father was "almost a professional hunter," an avocation that led him to dog training and to Cliff Overvold, one of the best trainers in the country. Norm soon became interested in black Labradors and golden retrievers. He became very involved and had two good dogs. In 1946, when he was sixteen, he sold a golden retriever, Pirate of Stonegate, for $750, which later paid for tuition for two years at Concordia College. In 1948 Norm made headlines—"Freshman Makes Dog Hobby Pay Way Through Concordia"—when he sold a young black labrador, Jet of Stonegate, for $2,000 to a buyer who flew from St. Louis to make the transaction.

While he was at Concordia, Norm was expected to work for the company. Most of the accounts were still done by hand, and there were always two people to balance every account. When that work was done, he was expected to do the janitorial duties. At that time the office staff consisted of Martin, Maurice, Agnes Foss, Marlys Powers, and Norm, who worked part-time as janitor and helped to do interest compilations on savings accounts twice annually. Marlys Powers recalled that her starting pay was $38 a week, and she was sure she "had the world by the tail."

From 1945 through 1948, because of the many contacts that they had made throughout the state, both Martin and Maurice were able to capitalize on a once-in-a-lifetime opportunity. Ulland Mortgage Company of Fergus Falls was an agent for John Hancock Life Insurance Company, which had repossessed a great deal of land that fell into default during the 1930s. Legislation specified that the companies had to dispose of that land within ten years. Both of the Joneses were able to sell a considerable amount of Ulland's land on which they received a commission and were able to acquire land for themselves, sometimes on very good terms. Norm recalled that one half-section Maurice acquired near Kindred, which was leased out on one-third share of the crop, had a bumper yield of flax that paid off half of the loan. Norm stated that it did not help Metro, but it helped both families survive and was key to Metro's eventual success.

Little did Norm realize that his part-time office job would lead to a turning point in his life. Eunice M. Skurdahl was born on a farm where six girls, three boys, and their parents relied on the proceeds of a quarter section (160 acres) for their livelihood. Only Eunice and four others were able to go to high school. They shared rides with the neighbors, and if the roads were impassable, they stayed in town. After high school Eunice helped on the farm because her two older brothers were in the military. She reminisced: "I would have given anything to have been able to go to Concordia but there was no way we could swing it." After the farm work was over in the fall, she attended Interstate Business College from October 1947 through March 1948; then she returned to the farm to help her father. After their service years, her brothers went to college and "Dad said he needed me." She continued to work on the farm until the fall of 1948 when she joined five other girls in the office of Dakota Transfer. "It was a difficult place to work." In the spring of 1949 she returned to the farm again, and at the end of the crop season she returned to Interstate to ask Mr. Fossum for another job. He replied, "You are just the girl for Maurice Jones."

She started work at Metro, which was located on Second Avenue and Broadway. There were "three girls" and Martin and Maurice. Agnes Foss was a stenographer and head of the office. "The atmosphere was so friendly, happy, and warm. When grandpa (Martin) came in, he was always humming or singing." Eunice said his favorite tunes were "The Little Brown Church in the Vale" and "Listen to the Mocking Bird." He was a great tease at the same time. Martin and Maurice had similar sounding voices and liked to fool people on the phone.

Many who worked at Metro commented that Maurice stressed that they should "always be respectful and the customer was always right. He was so good in explaining to the customers and employees." Eunice suggested that Maurice should have been a psychologist, for it was surprising how many people came to him for advice.

All of the early employees described a family-like atmosphere. The annual meetings were held in the employee lunch room in the basement, but in 1949, when the company attained its first million in assets, it had "a millionaires' dinner" at The Top of the Mart, the most upscale place in Fargo-Moorhead at that time. Christmas checks of $25 were given out. Marlys Powers recalled that on a couple of particularly hot summer days after the office was closed, all the girls were taken to the Jones' lake cabin for a swim and a picnic. "We had such fun." When Min had to serve at a big gathering at First Lutheran Church, "We were all volunteered to help out and we all thought that was great."

Eunice related that the office was small and everyone knew what was going on. She recalled how Norm was always very friendly to everyone, just like his father and grandfather. He had offered to give her a ride home several times but "I was very respectful and declined because my sister, who I was rooming with, said I shouldn't have anything to do with the boss' son. It was not proper and she wanted me to do what was proper. She said, 'Besides, they are rich.' Finally, Agnes Foss told me to accept a ride with him and she assured me that they were not rich."

Norm's father was a good friend of Don Fraser, Fargo postmaster and a colonel in the North Dakota National Guard. Norm said that it was not his idea, but when he was nineteen his dad suggested that he should join the Guard. Guard service included going to Camp Grafton for summer maneuvers, but when the Korean War started and his Guard unit was called up, Norm and Eunice decided to get married December 20, 1950. Soon the 164th Unit of the Chemical Corps went to Camp Rucker, Alabama. Norm did not enjoy that duty, and with the help of Colonel Fraser was transferred into the food service where they served about 400 non-commissioned officers. Apparently his work there was good, and he was sent to chef's leadership school after which he was put in charge of the officers' mess hall. He gained a great deal of leadership from that experience because he was involved in all the planning. "That was a great experience."

Eunice took a civil service exam and was immediately given work as a stenographer in the quartermaster corps. On his first leave home, Norm met a former officer from the Canine Corps who suggested he transfer to the Corps, which was being organized for the Korean War. Norm then was transferred to Fort Riley, Kansas, to work in the Canine unit. He said of that experience, "It was fun duty but not much of a learning experience because I had already done that with my dad." Eunice found a place to live by going door-to-door and then took a position at a savings and loan. They soon moved to Colorado Springs where Eunice again worked in a bank that had a drive-up teller. In addition to his military duties, Norm had a part-time job with the Humane Society to earn extra income.

Norm assessed his military service in this manner: "It gave Eunice and me a chance to be by ourselves and mature. It was not the military experience that helped as much as the socio-economic growth by living in different parts of the country that helped us." Eunice had a job almost immediately after arriving in each place they lived. She profited from meeting people in all walks of life and was able to save a considerable portion of her income, which enabled them to buy their first car, a Pontiac, which cost about $900. After the car was paid for, they still had about $700 in savings. Both Eunice and Norm were brought up in such a manner that they learned the value of a dollar.

Soon, Eunice was pregnant and housing in Fargo was scarce, but they took a bold step and decided to build a home. When they were home on leave several months before being discharged, they decided to buy a lot, but where would they get the money? The catch was that they had to have a lot paid for to secure a home loan. Norm was thinking ahead and did not want to use his low-interest G.I. loan at this time because he already had a bigger project in mind where he could use it to better advantage. They realized that neither of their parents could help, so Norm asked his grandmother, Birgit, if she had money that she would be willing to loan. On March 17, 1952, she loaned them $1,500 for a lot at 302 Twenty-first Avenue North in Fargo.

It was not until August 2007 that they found out where that money came from. Norman's sister, Mary Ellen, had gone through Birgit's memorabilia and discovered her savings book from First Federal Savings and Loan Association of Fargo. Birgit had opened an account with First Federal on March 6, 1939, and during the next fourteen years she deposited $19,652. On May 6, 1942, she made the largest single deposit of $1,574; most others were in the low to mid-100s. The mystery is, why did she have a personal account in another firm? Was it because her account could be insured by the FDIC? Notations in the booklet indicate most of the income came from rent on land that was acquired when Martin and Maurice were selling farms for Ulland Realty.

Norm and Eunice secured a $10,000 loan from Gate City because they did not want to face any conflict of interest that could have arisen if they had borrowed from Metro. Both Norm and Eunice provided a great deal of "sweat equity" in their first home.

Martin Jones kept working until the very last and most enjoyed doing appraisal work with his grandson, Norman.

He drew the plans for the house; then a contractor put in the foundation and the basement. Norm helped with the framing, and then he did all the finishing, including building the cabinets. Eunice was eight months pregnant but helped lay the insulation. She said of that experience, "Climbing up the steps into the attic— that was hard."

Eunice commented that Norm had often said that he had wanted to take up architecture. He was still not sure if he wanted to go to work for the company or continue in college. At this juncture Maurice told him that there was an opening in the company and if he did not come to work, he might lose out. Maurice had never tried to pressure Norm, but now he laid out the facts. Eunice commented, "So Norm went to work instead of continuing college and he has been a 'frustrated architect' ever since."

But the company was just beginning to grow. Norm reminisced, "We finally reached the $2 million mark in deposits. My dad and grandfather both said, 'This would be a good spot for you to come back to, if you want.'" He was only the sixth employee so he might have had some doubt about its future. He did everything from working as a teller to taking loan applications to running the posting machine. He enjoyed that job the most because he realized mathematics was a strength of his, but he also liked being a leader, which he attributed to his Boy Scout training.

After looking back on those years, Eunice commented that Maurice was a real motivator and Min was the greatest cheerleader, which made the young couple comfortable about joining Metro. But probably his most enjoyable work was when he went on appraisals with his grandfather. Martin was seventy-five but still spry enough to do that work. Eunice said, "His grandfather led by example and he was so experienced and gentle. He was the greatest influence on Norman's life. From that work Norman gleaned the ways of Martin." Eunice added, "This gave Norm a "real feel about appraising and how valuable it was to the business. It was a sound learning experience because grandpa was a good teacher." Norm was a real stickler about appraisals, and that served Metro well.[6]

∿　∿　∿　∿　∿

1.　Edmund Wrigley, *The Working Man's Way to Wealth: A Practical Treatise on Building Associations: What They Are and How to Use Them* (Philadelphia: James K. Simon, 1872), p. 5-6, hereafter Wrigley; Josephine Hedges Ewalt, *A Business Reborn: The Savings and Loan Story, 1930-1960* (Chicago: American Savings and Loan Institute Press, 1962), p. 4-7, 371-372, hereafter Ewalt; *Metropolitan Financial Corporation 1926-1995* (Fargo, privately printed, 1995), p. 3, hereafter *Metropolitan History.*

2.　Ewalt, pp. 15, 18, 27, 33, 55-56, 61, 79-80, 89, 101-102, 105; *Metropolitan History*, p. 3.

3.　David B. Danbom, *Going It Alone: Fargo Grapples with the Great Depression* (St. Paul: Minnesota Historical Society Press, 2005), pp. IX, 4, 98, hereafter Danbom; Sixteenth United States Census 1940, Population Volume II, Characteristics of the Population Part V, p. 425; Elwyn B. Robinson, *History of North Dakota* (Lincoln: University of Nebraska Press, 1966) pp. 376-377, hereafter Robinson.

4.　*Metropolitan History*, pp. 3-4; "Maurice H. Jones, One of Metropolitan's Founders in 1926," *Howard Binford's Guide* XI. No.6 (December 1978), pp.24, 44 hereafter Binford; *The Fargo Forum*, October 5, November 20, 1929, January 8, 21, 25, February 6, 9, December 19, 1930, March 5, September 12, 27, 1931; A tabulation of assets by year in Norman M. Jones file, hereafter tabulation of assets.

5.　Tabulation of assets; *The Fargo Forum*, September 27, 1931, January 1, 7, 17, 1932, July 7, 1933; Metropolitan History, pp. 4-6; *FMDirectory*, 1919,1924, 1938; Binford p. 24; Skurdall-Jones, p, 97-98; *Annual Report of Building and Loan*

Associations of the State of North Dakota 1940, letter of the state examiner to the governor and reports from 1930-1944, hereafter Annual Report; 1965 speech; data gathered from the Associations Annual Financial Statements issued to the members, hereafter Metropolitan Annual Report.

6. Interviews of Norman M. Jones, April 23, May 1, and additional conversations 2007, hereafter Norman Jones interview; interview of David Green, Lake Park, Minnesota, June 27, 2007, hereafter Green interview; Golberg interview, *The Fargo Forum*, September n.a. ,1948; interview of Eunice M. Jones, April 18, and additional conversations in 2007 and 2008, hereafter Eunice Jones interview; interview of Marlys Powers Anderson, August 13, 2007, hereafter Powers Anderson interview; a conversation with Min Jones (Mrs. Maurice), with the author, c.a. 1983; interview of Nancy Jones Schafer, Fargo, June 8, 2007, hereafter Schafer interview; interviews of Noel Fedje, Fargo, May 9, June 13, 2007, hereafter Fedje interview; *The Saint Paul Pioneer Press*, November 23, 1992.

Chapter III

Maurice H. Jones Builds a Firm Foundation 1953-1966

Maurice Jones, Everyone's Friend

Maurice was well trained before he assumed the presidency in 1953. He had worked side by side with his father Martin since 1926. There is no indication that there was anything but harmony between father and son, so we can only assume that Maurice saw no particular reason to encourage his father to step aside. He enjoyed a free hand during most of his years as an understudy and was satisfied to let his father enjoy his seventh decade of life as president. Those who knew Maurice realized being the president did not mean that much to him since he was, in practice, the captain of the ship.

Maurice was a well-liked person, had a wide range of interests, and was deeply involved in community affairs. A close friend commented,

> You would see Maurice and Min everywhere—at church, the country club, at the symphony ball. They cut a wide swath socially. Maurice and Martin were a good team in the business, but Maurice had more outside interests than either Martin or Norman. Maurice had golf, fishing, hunting, and raising dogs.

He served many positions at First Lutheran Church, including president. He chaired the Cass County American Red Cross Fund drives on more than one occasion, was district chair of the Red River Valley Boy Scouts of America, and was president of the Cosmopolitan Club and many other organizations. In business he

Maurice H. Jones, 1905-1971. He served Metropolitan from 1926 to 1970, during which time the Association and its leader became highly recognized in the industry.

was a director of the Federal Home Loan Bank of Des Moines, district twelve of the National Association, before he became president of Metropolitan. The Des Moines district included the two Dakotas, Iowa, Minnesota, and Missouri, and at that time had assets of more than $71 million. He served as president of the North Dakota Savings and Loan League, and was a board member of the United States Savings and Loan League. "He knew virtually every savings and loan executive in the country and was considered the dean of the savings and loan executives in North Dakota." Maurice was cautiously conservative in managing the affairs of the Association, and with Martin always in the wings, but not meddling, Maurice kept Metropolitan afloat and in better financial condition than most thrifts. That was the basis for much of the success enjoyed in later years.

Mike Nilles, whose family had a lifelong connection with Metro, related that in general the thrifts had closer relations with customers than the commercial banks. In this respect Metro had a distinct reputation as being customer friendly because of the Jones connection.

> Maurice, and later Norman, were both so well met. I remember my dad, John J., and Maurice really worked on this, and when my brother Bill joined he quickly inherited the same philosophy [as did] Norman, first with the customers and then others in the industry. This gave Metro a real heads-up position among S&Ls in the state and then nationally.

Bill Nilles, who started February 1, 1955, said, "Maurice was personality-plus. He could meet anyone and could converse about almost any subject. He was an excellent teacher and taught me most of what I know about the business. He was like a father to those of us in the office." Nancy Jones Schafer, who knew Maurice during the last three years of his life while she was courted by Maurice Jr., saw him as being so dignified and yet so humble. His zest for life was contagious. He never raised his voice and was kind to everyone. "We had a real comfort level and trust for each other." This was quite a contrast for Nancy, who grew up with a stoic father, in that she discovered what it was to have an affectionate father. "It gave me courage to change my relationship with my dad. I slept on the floor in his bedroom during the last five weeks of my father's life. Maurice's love for Jesus was very evident by the way he treated others, his family, and his church. Those three years were a real blessing to me." He had a compassion and generosity for people. He was a good judge of people too, which was apparent when dealing with customers who came to the office to plead for an extension or for another loan, for he could be lenient but he also knew when to say no.

Bill Nilles joined Metro in 1955 and quickly formed a close relationship with Norm that lasted for his entire career with the company. They were an exemplary leadership team.

Tony Renner was the tenth person on the staff when he came to work as the first full-time accountant on August 20, 1956. When he applied for the position, Maurice interviewed him, and on his second visit Bill and Norm interviewed him. He was twenty-eight years old at the time and no stranger to working for others. When asked to describe Maurice Jones, he replied, "He was the kindest person you could ever know." Then he told this story. "In October I asked Maurice if I could have a day off. He asked what for and I said to get married, and he said, 'Then you should take the whole week off with pay.' That sold me on the company."

Richard "Dick" Kvamme had two distinct relationships with Metro, first as a contractor who borrowed money to build houses and later as a board member. He was just starting his business and on a shoestring financially and was quite pleased with how he was treated by Maurice, "who made virtually all the key decisions." When he was named to the board, Kvamme was amazed at the exceptional way Maurice presented himself to that group. "He was so at ease in selling his ideas even when presenting something new or controversial. He was a real gentleman and a wonderful person to do business with." Kvamme recalled an incident in about 1960 when he was chairman of a fund drive for a Camp Fire Girls project. He asked Maurice for a donation and received a check. Then, Maurice suggested that he call on the bank across the street that Kvamme was not acquainted with. When he called on the bank there was a check ready for the same amount. That was a gift they would not have received otherwise.

Trueman Tryhus saw Maurice from two perspectives, first as a social friend and later as a board member. Tryhus quickly chose four words to describe his close friend: "Solid, trustworthy, kind, and benevolent." He said that in business matters, Maurice was not a risk taker because he had spent too many years struggling to keep Metro afloat to overcome some of the associated fears that he had felt during the 1930s. In the early 1960s, Tryhus and Norm formed a partnership to develop some real estate. They called it T and J Investment. Tryhus reminisced that Maurice confronted Norm and asked him if he wanted to work full-time or if he wanted to be an entrepreneur in development. "Norm came to me and asked if I would mind if I would buy him out. It was easy for me. Instead of Tryhus and Jones, it became Tryhus and Joan [his wife]."[1]

A Happy Working Environment

Metropolitan Building and Loan Association, like most small thrifts, lacked the capital to have its own building. From 1926 to 1955 it moved several times as it needed more space but always in the heart of Fargo. As stated previously, the Globe Building was only fourteen feet wide with two teller windows at the front; Maurice had a desk facing the public with Norm immediately behind him. Maurice specialized in loans and was always available to speak to anyone. Norm did everything, filling in wherever needed. Marlys

Powers said, "We were crowded in that building but no one really objected because we all enjoyed the setting."

The assets increased every year from $839,545 in 1943 to $$4,265,411 in 1953 with $226,400 in reserves and undivided profits. Metro had come through the 1930s, World War II, and the Korean War without a loss of a penny to any of its 7,000 depositors and borrowers. In preparation for a larger facility, a 100-x-150-foot lot, with houses, on Fifth Street and Third Avenue North was purchased. The houses were of low value and subsequently demolished. The lot was large enough for a building and a parking lot.

After Martin Jones died on July 7, 1954, Norm realized that the company probably was big enough to support another family. In any case, Norm "got the feeling" that he might like to make a career at Metro. Then, Bill Nilles came into the picture. (Because of the close association that these two had, henceforth "Bill" and "Norm" will be used. This is how all the interviewees referred to them and apparently was common usage throughout the company.) Norm's first comment about Bill, who became a confidant and lifelong business partner, was, "He was an interesting person, all business." After graduating from college, Bill had the same problem as Norm. He said, "I had no idea what I wanted to do. My dad, John J., was a director but I did not know a thing about the company. But Dad encouraged me to apply." Bill recalled that the first time he went into the Metro office in the Globe Clothing building he thought it was "crummy," but he was amazed at how upbeat the people were.

Since both Bill and Norm were veterans, they were eligible for on-the-job training under the G. I. Bill which supplemented any wages up to $310 per month. Norm's wife, Eunice, commented that the G.I. Bill was a real boon for Metro and Norm and Bill because they were started at $110 a month, which meant that the government paid $200 each month for the first year. In the second year the government paid $155, and in the third, $100. Maurice must have been impressed with Bill. After the first nine months, Bill lost the G.I. benefits because his salary was raised beyond the $310 maximum. Maurice simply told him he deserved more.

Soon after Norm started full-time, his father had suggested that they push for a better building. Maurice realized that it was time to build but he did not want to lead, so he told Norm, "If you want to grow the company bigger—do it yourself." Norm recalled, "From that day it was full speed ahead for a new building for me and Bill." Norm and Dick Kvamme, their contractor, traveled to look at the three new financial buildings in Pipestone, Minneapolis, and Willmar "to see what was really needed." They liked the one in Willmar. Kvamme went to the drafting board to design the building.

A brochure was prepared partially in memory of Martin Jones and partially about dedicating the new building and how it would provide better service. Norm, the first one of the third generation to work at Metro, was the master of ceremonies for the dedication. He commented about the event: "The excitement of planning the building and then being the emcee really got me enthused about staying with the company." He never forgot the compliment that Mike Nilles, Bill's brother, made after the event. Mike said, "You did a great job as emcee. I cannot believe that a man as young as you has become such an accomplished speaker."

Once Norm and Eunice made the decision to stay with Metro, they sold their house on Twenty-first Avenue North for $15,000 and applied those proceeds, along with Norm's G.I. loan benefits, to borrow money from Gate City again to build a four-unit apartment house. They remained there for only four years before they made a third move into another of the twenty-two properties they lived in during their career. Norm understood the housing market and the importance of sweat equity in building assets.

The new company office at Third Avenue and Fifth Street, including the lot, cost less than $200,000, plus the cost of an array of new labor-saving, error-reducing, and customer-friendly innovations that were introduced—window posting machines, which put the entries into the passbook and the ledger, and printed the dividends in a separate column simultaneously; a large vault for records and safety deposit boxes; a drive-up window; customer parking for twenty-five cars; a twenty-four-hour depository; and FSLIC insurance of $10,000 for each account. Dividends of 2.5 percent were paid on those accounts.

When the grand opening took place in December 1955, the place was filled with flowers. Then the crowd came. Bill recalled that there were cookies, coffee, and other goodies for everyone. The ladies received a bottle of perfume and the men, retractable cardboard box openers. As an added attraction, new premiums were

Groundbreaking for Metropolitan's first building on Third Avenue and Fifth Street, spring 1955. Left to right, R. J. Theis, Bill Nilles, Oscar Brekke, Mel Toussaint, Maurice Jones, Oscar Kjorlie, and Norman Jones.

Metropolitan moved from a fourteen-foot wide building with two teller windows to a lobby partially filled with four teller windows, which gave the feeling of spaciousness, yet was small enough to maintain a sense of community.

introduced. Metro had started using premiums in 1932 to entice new deposits, but the grand opening of its first building took the premium campaign to a new level. Agnes Foss, the senior employee outside of the family, had never liked working with the premiums, in part because she felt people opened new accounts just to get pots and pans for Christmas gifts. Bill said, "Oh, yes, then, those premiums. We were great on them. They were a nuisance but you cannot believe how they brought the money in." The premiums were such a success at the open house that they were pushed hard after that. One of the big hits as a premium was the Schafer ballpoint pen. That was followed by china plates, cups, and saucers until a full set of dishes was acquired. Later, stone-made china became popular, and after that Wearever pots and pans were offered.

Splendid as the new building was, they soon found flaws. The basement flooded several times. Initially, Bill was the first to be called if there was a problem. Dan and John Quello, sons of the Rev. Julius Quello of First Lutheran, were the janitors. They had to come down after storms several times to drain and mop up the basement. One time things were particularly bad and their father came down to help. Fortunately, that problem was quickly solved. Bill was called frequently because the burglar alarm kept going off until they realized that it was set off by the night police officer's flashlight.

Marlys Powers recalled that everything was shut down in preparation for using the weekend to move into the new building. "We were like sardines in the old building and we could not believe all the space we suddenly had; we got all kinds of new machines." The office was still small enough that everyone was still expected to fill in wherever there was a need. "We were one big family and it was fun." Bill was assigned to work as a lending trainee, which required typing loan papers, but he was not good at typing so he was sent to Interstate Business College for a course to upgrade his skills. After the new building was finished, he sometimes had to step in as a teller to take deposits.

To attract young savers there was a special teller window with two steps for small children. Next to it was a sucker tree. Small piggy banks that were shaped like a book came in a variety of colors and were popular and very effective in getting young savings accounts. Many tellers recalled taking deposits of less than a dollar, and the average deposit from those banks ran from $1.25 to $3. There was a key at each teller's window for opening the banks. The job of taking the deposits from "piggy" banks was made easier when coin counters were purchased in 1955.

Everyone worked as late as necessary on December 31 when the annual statement was prepared and mailed. The envelopes were ready, and as soon as the printer brought the statement, it was inserted into the envelope along with a small calendar and delivered to the post office so it could be postmarked January 1.

After being exposed to every position in the office, Bill made his first loan. It was for $7,500 at 6 percent for twenty years on a house in Fargo. Norm had gone through the same routine; he was the lone appraiser of this property. During the 1950s, Metro started making many construction loans that really increased its business because many of these loans were assumed by the home buyer.

Tony Renner was impressed with the roomy new office all on one floor with a basement for a staff lunch room and another room that Maurice had specifically requested. This community room was a first for the city. It held up to 150 people for meetings and 100 for luncheons and was available for customers and community organizations. The drive-up window was also a first in the area, and customers were not acquainted with using one, so initially it was not busy. Tony's desk was near that window and he frequently waited on customers because the tellers were all busy with others who preferred to park and walk in to make their deposits. Some days only six to twelve cars would drive up to it. But after a few months it became popular and had to be manned full-time. There was no trouble getting tellers to work at the drive-up because it was still a novelty.

One morning the big posting machine would not work. It was new to everyone in the office and no one offered any help, so Tony called the Burroughs repairman. He found the trouble promptly—it was not plugged in. A very shy Tony said, "I was embarrassed."

Nearly all employees other than Bill and Norm who were employed during the 1940s and 1950s were from farms, and most had not been away from their home community for any length of time when they came to Fargo-Moorhead to take a year or two of business college. Tony Renner, who came from south-central North Dakota, did farm work for four years after high school, then was in the service for three years, after which he attended a business college.

Joan Horn came from a farm near Pine River, Minnesota—not the best farming region—to attend Dakota Business College. She received some help from her parents and worked at the home of F.L. Watkins, the president of the school, for her room and board. She remembered how frightened she was on the day in June 1957 when she was interviewed by "Mr. Maurice" (Jones) and he asked her if she smoked. She was relieved to say no. Her fright was soon allayed because he was so kind and easy to converse with. She interviewed for the position as receptionist and was thrilled to be offered the position for $180 a month. She said, "Mr. Jones was so approachable and a real team builder. The first thing he did was to give instructions on how to answer the phone." He reminded her how important that was because it was the first contact the public had with the company. In addition to answering the phone she was also assigned to greet the walk-in customers. When not busy with those duties, she took dictation and typed letters. Joan was probably the last secretary who used shorthand for—according to Tony Renner, who was responsible for modernizing the office equipment—dictaphones were purchased soon after she came to work. They proved to be time and labor savers.

Joan said, "I could not have asked for a better job." She enjoyed the special treat of going to the Jones' cabins in the summer and learning to water ski. "Min and Eunice would put on the best dinners." Bill and Norm got the idea soon after they moved into the new building that Metro should advertise on television. Joan was assigned to bring a greeting from the company and then the forecaster gave the weather. This added publicity on the new media promoted recognition of Metro, and business increased rapidly.

Norm gave serious attention to what was being put on the air; he had a good feel for the people Metro did business with and knew what would appeal to them. One day David Green, Norm's closest friend from grade and high school days, received a call to come to the office to listen to a jingle that a Chicago ad agency had written. Norm did not like it and asked Dave to write another one. That was the start of Dave's part-time work while teaching French at Concordia College. In addition to writing jingles, he also made layouts and other marketing materials.

Betty Ihry had finished a year at a business college in the spring of 1958 when Metro called the school. Betty was interviewed by

Maurice and two days later he called and asked her if she smoked. "I said yes. He said no one else in the office smoked so he hesitated." When the six girls in the office asked him why he did not hire Betty, he replied that she smoked. Smoking had become the rage of young women at this period, and three of them confessed that they smoked. Everyone in the office pleaded with Maurice, "Go ahead and hire her." That was the start of her illustrious twenty-seven-year career with Metro.

Betty had two interruptions in her career, first to be with her husband in the military in Germany and another for the birth of a son. She never had any doubt about returning to Metro because "they always made me promise that I would return. The family was so great to work with so there was never a doubt." The annual party was held at restaurants, but in the summer they nearly always had parties at Maurice's or Norm's cabins.

The company expanded rapidly at this time. The economy was good, television advertising was very effective, and updating equipment speeded up customer service. The office routine was not even disturbed one day when a trainee was on an errand to take the money bag to deposit at the bank. She stopped at the Novelty Shop and set the money bag down while she looked around. When she got to the bank, she realized what she had done. In the meantime the shop manager had put the bag behind the counter, knowing that someone would come for it. The trainee who had misplaced the bag was too shaken to return to the shop and take it to the bank. Another girl did, and management never knew what had taken place.

In 1959 Concordia College art professor Cy Running was commissioned to do a mural on the wall behind the tellers. The mural depicted agriculture, mining, and oil wells, the major industries of North Dakota, along with a city and a rural landscape. This was a big attraction to an already-appealing building.

Bev Thompson Vandrovec was seventeen when she graduated from Lisbon High School, so she could only get a job as a bookkeeper with a small firm that was not concerned about the age limitation. After she turned eighteen, she walked into Metro unannounced to apply because she heard that it was such a great place to work. Maurice informed her that they were not looking for help at the time, but "he interviewed me anyway and then said he would find a place. I think he hired me because I was from Lisbon." Bev said,

A portion of the fifty-foot long mural that has been preserved and is on a wall of the board room of the R.D. Offutt Company office in the Island Park area of Fargo.

At Third and Fifth we were one happy family. We would stop to buy rolls for afternoon coffee when all gathered in the lunch room. Maurice was so thoughtful. One day he knew I had been working bending over the posting machine and came over and rubbed my back. That felt so good—but I suppose today that would be forbidden. He was like a dad and praised you regularly. But the Joneses all made us feel like family.

Bev related how often it was stressed that regardless how small or large the problem, the customer was always right. She felt that the customers reciprocated because "every once in awhile I would get a box of candy or other gifts from a customer."

The Norm and Bill team came into the business at an exciting time, and they were quick to take advantage of the situation. Norm, like his predecessors, Martin and Maurice, always kept an eye on Gate City. Maurice and Norm noted that Gate City had added branches in Bismarck and Minot and both were doing very well. It occurred to them that maybe Metro should look for an opportunity to do the same. Maurice was satisfied with the progress of the company and did not have the entrepreneurial spirit that Norm had,

67

but he told Bill and Norm, "If you want to work that hard, go ahead." Norm realized that his father was interested in growth and thought that some day he would like to be as big as Gate City, so he willingly went along with their plans but suggested the branches be near Fargo, preferably in the Red River Valley. Maurice was in his fifties and was content to grow Metro at a steady, solid pace. By 1959 the company had 8,000 members, assets had grown to $16.5 million, the dividend rate had increased to 3.5 percent paid semi-annually, and accounts were insured up to $10,000.

The Jones family was very well known and had a good reputation in Richland County, a prime agricultural area. Martin Jones had a wide following in the county, so Maurice, Norm, and Bill all agreed that Wahpeton would be the logical site for a branch. Then, Maurice suggested that a local advisory board should be established for the purpose of tying Metro into the community, which proved to be very effective. The Wahpeton board was made up of Selmer Jordheim, a prominent farmer; Bryce Smith, owner and operator of Smith Motors; Virgil Sturdevant, owner of a small chain of auto parts stores and mayor of Wahpeton; and Jimmy Little, a well-known insurance agent and realtor from Wyndmere. They gave Metro a solid base of local connections. In the early years Norm, and later his brother, Morrie, always tried to make the monthly meetings. On July 1, 1959, Clarence Bladow—who had worked in a Wahpeton bank for eight years, was well known, and had an excellent reputation as a banker—was employed as the branch manager.

Plans were made for an office capable of accommodating $40 million in assets. The office was opened August 1, 1959, with Bladow and one assistant and became an immediate success. The brochure announcing its opening stated that the air-conditioned building, which was still a novelty in small-town offices, would have three teller windows and a special children's window. It also had a community room, which was recommended by Maurice to enhance the tie to the local community. This became a very popular meeting place and later was in such demand that it had to be booked far in advance.

A customer base was developed by giving premiums for opening new accounts, everything for the home—pots and pans, china, stoneware, silverware, wrist watches, fountain pens, luggage of all sizes and types, and television sets. Meanwhile, banks were prohibited by regulations from using premiums. This particularly irked the banks, which traditionally had not been friends of the S&Ls. There was a restriction on what the premiums could cost, but by buying large quantities the per-item cost was very low so people could get good bargains on blankets, Corning ware, and similar items. Many people from the area west of Wahpeton—people who were not bank customers nor patronized the local independent banks that had no competition—were attracted by the premiums and opened accounts at Metro. See Chapter Four for more details about the variety and impact of premiums.

Bladow commented about a person from Dazey, about 120 miles to the northwest but had relatives near Wahpeton, who drove a very old car. He came in and wanted to meet with Bladow in the office, with the door shut, and asked several times if his money would be safe if he deposited there. Bladow assured him that it was insured and would be perfectly safe. Then, the man opened a container, which had about $6,000 in it, that had been kept in his house so long that it was "very smelly." Receiving money with a musty smell happened often those days, especially from older individuals who had experienced the bank failures of the 1930s. On another occasion a man rode up on horseback and left the horse standing along the curb while he came in to open an account.

Wahpeton proved to be a gold mine. By 1963 it had four employees. Deposits increased rapidly, providing funds for loans in Fargo that spurted Metro's growth. Wahpeton grew to over $100 million in deposits, which was larger than the two local banks combined. Only about $25 million was needed for local loans, so the other $75 million was available for loans in Fargo or where needed. Later, that changed when Wahpeton had a housing spurt and the demand for home loans increased in the community. In its first fifteen years, the Wahpeton office financed over 2,300 homes and had grown to over 13,000 savings account customers.

Bladow, who had never done any appraising in his previous work, recalled that Norm came from Fargo to teach him the basics. The loans had to get approval from the home office, but that was not a deterrent, for within a decade they were making more home real estate loans than any of the community banks. An insurance department and a mobile home department were added.

The success at Wahpeton encouraged a search for locations for additional branches. The economy was very good in North Dakota during the 1970s, so the new branches did not experience financial difficulties. Even though they did not grow as rapidly as Wahpeton, they still had a positive cash flow.

Norm attended savings and loans graduate courses at the University of Indiana, Bloomington, during 1959, 1960, and 1961. He said of that experience, "It made me think about long-range planning. The seminars reinforced what we had been doing, which was a real confidence builder for me. Bill was running the ship while I was gone and Dad was so supportive of the ideas we came up with." Tony Renner reflected, "Those specialized courses honed Norm's natural entrepreneurial talents and strengthened the Bill and Norm team. Bill was all business and always on top of things while Norm was thinking ahead—the real visionary."[2]

A Home Loan Leads to a Change in Life

On May 15, 1956, after graduating from college and spending three years in the military, Doug Larsen opened a Ben Franklin Store in Northport, a new mall in north Fargo. In the summer of 1957, he and his wife, Sally, decided they wanted to build a house. They already owned a lot, so Doug went to Merchants National Bank where he had his business account and, armed with his G.I. Loan Certificate, applied for a loan to build. He was turned down because the bank felt that his business was not progressing well enough. After a few days he went to Gate City Building and Loan, where he had a savings account of $500 that had come from wedding gifts, and received his second turn-down.

Doug recalled:

> My parents protested because they felt that one should not borrow money for anything except for business purposes. So they were no help. But Sally and I wanted a house, but I did not know where to go. After being turned down twice for financing, I turned to Dick Kvamme, who we had contracted to build the house, and he introduced us to Metropolitan. Our lot was worth $775, and with the $500 in wedding cash plus my G.I. certificate, Metropolitan agreed to make a loan for $16,000. The interest was 4.25 percent making the payment $67.50 per month. I got the impression that the other firms did not like to build according to the G.I. requirements.

Doug was eager to tell rest of the story. He and Trueman Tryhus had been classmates at Casselton. Tryhus had gone to college to become a dentist and established his practice in Fargo. He became a member of First Lutheran where the Joneses also attended. Doug had only met Norm briefly when they got the loan. It was not long before Tryhus and Doug came up with the idea that they should take one afternoon off each week to play golf. Tryhus got Norm and Ralph Rudrud, also a First Lutheran member, to join them.

Doug commented that Norm was not a good golfer because his attention span was too short. His mind was always on business or something that the church could be doing. But this was the start of a golf foursome that became known as the "Norwegian Legion." Doug said, "I had to remind Norman that the game was not a First Lutheran Council meeting. He never got down to talking golf until at least the fifth hole."

Doug and Sally Larsen were good business people. Within a few years their Ben Franklin business was thriving, and they added other stores. One day in 1966 Norm called him to the Metropolitan office because he and his father wanted to talk to him. In the conversation Doug learned that Maurice had visited with board member Gene Paulson of Epko Films, where Doug had worked while going to high school because he wanted to learn more about photography. Fortunately for Doug, Paulson appreciated his ability and work habits. When Oscar Kjorlie, one of the first directors of Metropolitan, died, Paulson suggested that Maurice consider Doug as a replacement on the board.

Doug's initial reaction when Maurice and Norm asked him to serve on the Metro board was that he knew nothing about finance. The Joneses knew better because they knew how well his business was doing. Once again Doug's father objected because being on the board would take time away from the store. Doug's initial reaction was to decline, but after he learned that he would receive $150 (about $2,200 in 2007 dollars) for one afternoon meeting a month, he had a change of heart. The Larsens grew up living frugally. In 1957 when they opened the Ben Franklin Store, he and Sally agreed to a $200-per-month withdrawal from the business for family needs. That figure did not change until 1966 when it was increased to $300 per month when he joined the Metro board.

Doug said, "The decision to take a position on the board changed my life. We used that money to do things for the family, which was a boon for all five of us." But more importantly, he saw how ethical the Jones family was in how they operated Metropolitan. He said, "I enjoyed and appreciated that. I felt a sense of improved self esteem in the community because of the good will that the family had in their home area and industry wide."[3]

Passing the Baton

On January 1, 1946, after holding the office of assistant secretary since 1926, Maurice Jones Sr. was elected secretary and manager. There was no perceivable change in operations, for once he had proven himself, his father had basically let him have free reign in managing the business. On January 1, 1953, he succeeded his seventy-seven-year-old father, Martin, as president of the company. The father and son team had guided Metro through the 1930s and beyond without losing a penny that was entrusted to them; they were on solid ground to take it into the prosperous years that followed. Maurice felt confident about the opportunities ahead.

In July 1955 the company had 7,000 member savers and home owners. The dividend rate was 2.5 percent per year. It had a new building with one of the few drive-up teller windows in the northwest and a twenty-five-car parking lot. Its reserves had grown to $286,000 and assets to $7.2 million. The usually all-business-like Bill Nilles was elated when he expressed that deposits had hit $6 million. "We had a dinner at the FM [the new Moorhead hotel] to celebrate the event." In a brochure dated September 24, 1955, Maurice wrote,

> There is no better security on earth for your savings than selected, monthly reducing first mortgages on homes. Metropolitan has a large portion of its funds invested in these fine homes in our community. [The] American home is the safeguard of American liberties.

It was not publicly expressed, but insiders noted that the company had risen to the number three spot among the thrifts in Fargo and was growing at a much faster rate than its competitors in Fargo and out-state communities. Metro's growth in assets was nearly double one of its Fargo competitors. The statewide picture was even brighter. Fargo was the largest and most rapidly growing city in the state. This put it in a position to overcome the outlying thrifts because industrialization of agriculture was causing a decline in farm numbers and thus, a declining rural population. This decline accelerated in the 1950s and has continued.

Norm and Bill were becoming a solid team, and Maurice gave them the freedom to move ahead just like he had received from his father. Maurice held the reins but in a loose manner. Norm and Bill were like spirited horses at the starting gate and were in the right spot at a most opportune time. Norm was the idea person with a real vision, but if Bill could not make the numbers work, the proposal was usually dropped.

In 1963 nearly half of thrifts nationwide had assets of less than $5 million, and the industry average was $17 million. That year Metro had assets of $34.9 million and reserves of $1.6 million and was the third largest savings and loan in North Dakota. The success at Wahpeton was so positive that Norm and Bill immediately started searching for another opportunity. Even though it would cost up to $100,000 to open a new branch office, the company was in a strong enough position to risk the cost. Metro hoped that it could open the second branch in Grand Forks, but the banking commission, which was made up of bankers, denied their request. So it was decided to locate at Grafton, a community with a solid agricultural base. On September 1, 1963, Metro opened a second branch there. It was not as prosperous as Wahpeton but it had potential because of its nearness to Grand Forks.

Savings customers increased from 13,500 in 1962 to 14,700 in 1963. Part of the increase in new customers came as a result of the branch at Grafton. The cost of the new office reduced reserves by $100,000, but it appeared the opportunity could not be passed up. Norm and Bill were ecstatic, for greater horizons were open, and by December 8, 1963, the first sketch of the new building was available.

The timing was great. In 1963 the nation's thrifts had total assets of $183 billion in loans, of which $79.1 billion was loaned on one- to four-family homes. Metro had 90 percent of its savings capital invested in first mortgages in owner-occupied homes or farm acreages, i.e. small farms located near cities where the owners had a second occupation so they were primarily rural residents. Virtually all of these small operations were located in the Red River Valley, which reflected the nationwide trend of farm consolidation.

Between 1960 and 1970, the savings and loan industry grew by $89 billion, which was fostered by a solid economic environment with minimal competition and stable interest rates. Then the economy changed, which caused a decline in savings because the cost of money to the industry increased and many of the thrifts were unable to adapt their portfolios to meet the changes. Part of the problem was that the small thrifts were not professionally managed and were too reliant on a single-industry local economy.[4]

A New Office in the Tower

A new horizon opened in February 1961 after the company purchased a lot across the street to the south of their location from the Urban Renewal Agency for $50,000. Fargo continued to thrive and grow, and Metropolitan prospered with it. By 1963 the structure erected in 1955 at Third Avenue and Fifth Street North was no longer adequate to handle the business. It was originally planned to handle $40 million annually, and it had exceeded that volume.

On May 2, 1964, groundbreaking for the new building on the lot at Fifth Street and Third Avenue North took place. On August 22nd, it was announced that the eight-story building would rise 104 feet above the sidewalk. Metropolitan would occupy the ground floor, which would be two stories high and include a mezzanine. The top six stories would be leased to tenants. On September 6, 1965, the company opened the $1,079,689 new building. It had $42 million in savings with $1.6 million in reserves when it moved into the new building.

Open house was held from September 27 to October 1, 1965. Jake Mauer, popular doorman at the Elks Club who had the reputation of knowing everyone in town, was the greeter for all who came. There was a gift for everyone—perfume, "Metro-Glo" night lights, plastic spin tops, and yardsticks—plus tables of food. Those who opened savings accounts of $200 or more received a West Bend Teflon-Finish Fry Pan. No transaction necessary—just sign up for the grand prize, a 1966 RCA Victor twenty-five-inch color television.

Tony Renner stated that Norm and Bill were given a "rather free hand on this project." Maurice realized that they were steering

The eight-story building dedicated September 1965—only ten years after the company's first building was opened—after a period when assets had grown nearly seven fold.

the ship into the future in great fashion. This gave him the freedom to concentrate on the day-to-day operations of the fast-growing company and at the same time spend much of his time out of the office making new contacts, a task he excelled at.

Bev Vandrovec expressed the consensus of the office staff: "We enjoyed the old building. We were crowded, which gave it a real family atmosphere. It was kind of sad moving into the new place, which was so much roomier, and you could almost sense that the family atmosphere lessened." However, those who had worked in other company offices disagreed. Betty Ihry stated: "Maurice still set the tone in the office. He was unbelievably wonderful, which created a great atmosphere, and even with the larger office, we still were one big family." When Betty returned in 1968, she was assigned to type mortgage papers and open new saving accounts when needed.

The entire office staff was on the ground floor; the Mezzanine was used for storage and the employee lounge. The cafeteria, the Metro Club, and a conference room were on the second floor. The cafeteria served coffee and noon lunches to Metro employees and all the employees of the firms that leased the top six floors. Occasionally customers were taken to the cafeteria or the conference room for a more relaxed setting and a cup of coffee and a cookie while, or after, doing business. The cafeteria was leased out on a percentage basis and was open to the public, but most of the business was from workers and customers of the tenants.

Shortly after moving into tower office, Dave Green produced a commercial—Café d' Paree—which proved very catchy and popular. He felt so good about it that he wanted to leave his teaching job and go full-time with Metro, but Norm understood his friend well enough to know that teaching was his field and discouraged him. In the late 1960s Beverly Cabezal (later Austin), who was on the air with Channel 4, was employed to handle public relations full-time. She went on to have a very successful career with the company.

Even though many new machines and innovations were adopted while in the office at Third and Fifth, most of the equipment was updated when the move was made to the tower. Probably the most striking was going online with the teller machines, which helped save time, but more importantly it reduced human error. Metro connected with the Federal Home Loan Bank service center in Des Moines. As new branches were opened, employees were brought in for training. Each branch office was wired into the system as soon as the technology was available, and branch employees were able to contact their appropriate home office when they had a problem.

Dorothy Kellerman worked at various jobs from 1942 to 1960 when she was employed at one of the local banks. Dorothy liked her job at the bank, but over the years she met many people from Metro who all talked about how great it was there. Most of these people had checking accounts at the bank because savings and loans did not offer that service yet. Tony Renner was one of them, and one day Dorothy commented that she would like to work at Metro. The only opening then was checking things in and out of the vault. Tony said that even though that was a very critical position, it might be a bit dull. A few days later Tony called Dorothy and said there was an opening for savings councilors, which involved opening new savings accounts from "piggy banks to the very largest CDs."

She stated, "I was impressed with Metro from the first day I was there and it never changed." Maurice Jones was not around much by that time, but "he and his wife Min were so kind and they were that way all the time to everyone." When she started in 1969, there were four employees in savings and six tellers. People were always directed to an individual savings counselor so she got to know her customers.[5]

∿　∿　∿　∿　∿

1. Binford,, p. 24; *The Nineteenth Annual Report of Federal Home Loan Bank of Des Moines*, April 23, 1952, hereafter FHLB 1952; interviews of Noel Fedje, Fargo, May 10, June 13, 2007, hereafter Fedje interview; interview of Michael " Mike" Nilles, Minneapolis, May 31, 2007, hereafter Mike Nilles interview; Schafer interview; interview of Tony Renner, Moorhead, May 7, 2007, hereafter Renner interview; interview of Richard Kvamme, Moorhead, April 11, 2007, hereafter Kvamme interview; interviews of Bill Nilles, Lake Park, Minnesota, March 19, June 27, 2007, hereafter Bill Nilles interview; interview of Trueman Tryhus, Fargo, May 18, 2007, hereafter Tryhus interview.
2. Bill Nilles interview; Norm Jones interview; Kvamme interview; Power Anderson interview; Metropolitan brochure September 24, 1955, hereafter September 1955 brochure; Mike Nilles interview; Skurdall-Jones, p. 98; Renner interview; interview of Joan Horn, Fargo, March 20, 2007, hereafter Horn interview; Green interview; Golberg interview; interview of Betty Ihry, Lake Park, Minnesota, March 19, 2007, hereafter Ihry interview; interview of Bev Thompson Vandrovec, Fargo, March 20, 2007, hereafter Vandrovec interview; interview of Clarence Bladow, Richville, Minnesota, May 8, 2008, hereafter

Bladow interview; *Metro Line (aka Metroline or Newsline)* the company newsletter, October 1978, May 1979, in possession of Mr. Bladow who has copies from 1974 through 1985, hereafter *Metro Line*; Norman Jones interview; *Metropolitan Financial Corporation*, 1926-1995, p. 8, hereafter *Metro History*; Norman Jones , *Savings and Loan Associations in the Future*, Graduate School Essay, University of Indiana , 1960, hereafter Jones 1960 Essay.

3.   A typed manuscript in the Norman Jones file; interview of Douglas Larsen, Fargo, May 4, 2007, hereafter Doug Larsen interview; Kvamme interview; Tryhus interview.

4.   Jones 1960 Essay; Eunice Jones interview; Renner interview; *Fargo Forum*, December 8, 1963, May 2, August 22, 1964, September 26, 2007; Power Anderson interview; Binford, p. 24; Vandrovec interview; Ihry interview; interview of Dorothy Kellerman, Fargo, May 24, 2007, hereafter Kellerman interview.

5.   Bill Nilles interview; *Metro History*,pp. 7, 10, 11; Bladow interview; Wahpeton Brochure 1959; Fedje interview; Skurdall-Jones, p. 99; Annual report 1955, 1956; North Dakota Savings and Loan Association Assets 1967 to 1984, hereafter NDS &LA Assets; Mike Nilles interview; Jones typed manuscript of acquisitions, hereafter acquisitions.

Chapter IV

A Visionary Takes Charge 1967-1982

On January 1, 1967, Norman Jones was elected president of the company. A news article coinciding with the announcement stated that the Federal Savings and Loan Insurance Corporation (FSLIC) decreed that insurance on all accounts be increased to $15,000. The company paid 4.5 percent dividend on regular passbook accounts, 5 percent on six-month investment certificates of deposit of $5,000, and 5.25 percent on $10,000 deposits. At the end of 1966, Metro had assets of $52.3 million up from only $7.2 million in 1955 when it moved into the new building on Third Avenue and Fifth Street and $16 million at the close of the 1950s.

Norman M. Jones, The New Leader

Everything appeared rosy until April 1966 when it was learned that Maurice Jones Sr. had cancer. To those who did not know all the details, it probably appeared that thirty-seven-year-old Norm was stepping into his sixty-two-year-old father's shoes a little early. This is particularly so since Martin Jones had held the presidency until he was seventy. In the fifteen years that Norm had been with the company, he had started by doing "grunt work" and climbed the corporate ladder quite rapidly. Metro was still a small company, but it was growing at a good pace so promotions came rapidly, particularly since the company preferred to promote from within. In 1953 Norm was named assistant secretary. In 1954 Richard J. Thies, one of the early directors, suggested that he should retire to make a position on the board for Norm, and that happened. In 1960 he became vice president and secretary, and in 1967, president.

Norman Jones was thirty-seven when he assumed the presidency because cancer forced his father to step down. His leadership began just as the savings and loan industry was about to enter a prolonged crisis. During the years that followed, Norm became a national financial figure and Metro experienced a meteoric rise.

Norm expressed gratitude that his father lived four years after it was known that he had cancer for it gave Norm more time to learn from him. Fortunately, Maurice was able to work until his final four months. He went moose hunting in three of his last four years. In the fall of 1969 Maurice was posted on the edge of a duck slough near Langdon while the others walked the area. When they returned Maurice had four ducks. They had flown off the slough and he hit all four. Norm said, "He was such a good shot."

David Green, Norm's grade school buddy, said that he was not aware of Norm's depths even though they were the closest of pals. After

Green was employed by Metro, he realized how intense Norm had become, even on the ski slopes. Green reminisced, "Whatever he did, he devoted himself 105 percent. He does so much for others and he has become so creative." Working closely with Norm, Green realized how important faith was in whatever he did, and he was so trustworthy.

Trueman Tryhus, a friend of more than fifty years, commented that when he first met Norm, the company was the smallest of the four thrifts in Fargo, which really challenged his competitive spirit.

He was just brimming with ideas, and I don't think there was an organization in the community that he did not chair. He was a real visionary, and most of the time he was on target. If he was wrong, he nearly always spotted the problem and quickly changed his focus.

Allen Golberg, another long-time friend, related that one of Norm's key traits was that he was a real decision maker. He could decide and then do it, and in the process he knew how to make changes without antagonizing people. Golberg added, "Eunice was the perfect person for him." Noel Fedje, long-time Fargo businessman, compared Norm to Wheelock Whitney, a well-known and respected Minnesota entrepreneur: "Neither was a great scholar, but both had great people skills, excelled at listening, and absorbed information. Norman surrounded himself with solid people that he could bounce ideas on. This was particularly true of his board."

When Norm was asked to explain the cause of dramatic growth from 1955 into the 1960s he replied:

The new building—people appreciated seeing the solid structure with black granite over the front entrance and a neon light showing the eagle on the FDIC insurance sign— and we were able to insure accounts up to $10,000. Dad was involved in the community, which gave us lots of exposure, and Bill and I were in the office to meet the new generation of borrowers and depositors. It was the beginning of television and we were the first savings and loan in the area to use television as our major media; we sponsored the weather broadcast on WDAY television. We really stepped up our advertising. We were the smallest in town so we had to try harder, and we really stressed putting the customer first.[1]

Bill and Norm, a.k.a. Salt and Pepper

In the process of writing books I have interviewed hundreds of people, many were business partners—some had excellent relationships and others experienced bitterness. But I can state without any hesitation that the relationship between these two men was about as near perfect as two people could have had. They were both men of great faith. Trueman Tryhus said that the relationship between Bill and Norm was

> so basic—Bill was so sharp with numbers and really understood the finance industry. But he was terrified with the thought of failures [meaning bad loans and acquisitions]. Bill could put the details together. Entrepreneurs like Norman are not hands-on managers. They want to create and do not want to concern themselves about the hands-on operation. Norm had perfect faith in Bill's ability to solve the challenge.

Bill's talents were recognized early, and he, too, rose rapidly up the corporate ladder. He started as loan trainee and did whatever had to be done in the office so he knew how the business functioned. After the usual training period, he concentrated on making loans. He recalled that the biggest house loan he was involved with was for $450,000 (which would be at least $3 million today based on the 2008 CPI data) in Phoenix to a North Dakota farmer from near Jamestown. In 1957 Bill was elected treasurer; in 1964 he was named vice president; the following year he was elected to the board of directors; and in 1971 he became senior vice president and secretary. After Maurice Jones retired, Bill and Norm were the top two people, and they became "very close." Everyone in the company marveled at how well they functioned as a team.

Metro enjoyed a period of years of uninterrupted growth. The banks continued to focus on commercial loans, which generally were larger, and let the thrifts have the home loans, which tended to be smaller and safer than the commercial business. As Metro grew larger, it gradually entered the commercial field. Bill recalled, "Then the regulations changed and competition became more intense."

A board member stated that if an issue had to do with the investment portfolio, they tended to follow what Bill suggested, and if the issue was over marketing or expansion, they followed Norm. "At no time did the board ever sense even a sniff of a clash between the two. That was not in Norman's makeup. There is no one in my life that had a more level demeanor. Only twice in the fifty years I have known him did he ever come close to being disturbed or unhappy." He continued: "The board was a hands-on working group, but Norm was never intimidated by a strong board. He never stopped learning. He got a kick out of the fact that he could zero in and get the answer to a problem from anyone."

This writer recalled seeing Norm come home at noon one day, put on his skis, and head for the ice-covered Red River. About twenty minutes later he returned, seemed very relaxed, and returned to the office. Later that day I remarked to him that there must have been pressure at the office, and judging from his smile, I sensed that he had found the solution.

In 1967 Mike Nilles, son of board member John and brother of Bill, became the lead company attorney. He recalled that people in the industry had been in the habit of calling Maurice to get his interpretation of changing regulations, which seemed to number from five to ten every month. Soon after Norm took over, they called him. Mike said, "Changes came so fast that I don't know how the industry would have been able to keep up with the changes without the computer."

Gary Dietz, an area branch supervisor also involved with mortgage lending, noted that Norm never had to "lean" too much on anyone if there was a problem.

> He knew how to ask questions without offending. Some of his ideas were off the wall, but Bill Nilles had a way of bringing him back to reality, always letting Norm lead the way because he and everyone on the top knew Norm would always find how to do things in the proper way.

It was almost a joke to board members that Bill seemed programmed to say no to Norm's new ideas. A board member commented,

> I am sure that if Bill had been in charge, Metro would not have grown as it did because he was so conservative.

Norman was conservative in a sense of being a good steward, always looking for ways to cut cost to keep the company in a profit mode. He never stopped keeping an eye on Gate City because it stayed ahead of us.

This board member thought that it was good that Metro never acquired Gate City because the competition was good motivation.

Bill, sitting in a wheelchair suffering from arthritis that had plagued him for most of his life, reminisced:

> They called us the salt and pepper team; Norm was the idea man and my job was to shoot holes in his plans. I was more practical. Norm was a shrewd loan person. We probably were too conservative and maybe should have taken more risks. We had a very low repossession ratio. [We] should have taken more chances. If I ever made a decision while Norm was out, he never once reversed what I did.

Norm proved that he was not only capable of managing other people's funds by guiding Metro along the road to success, but he also was enough of an entrepreneur that he was willing to venture with borrowed funds to improve his own portfolio. In 1965 Dick Kvamme, Trueman Tryhus, and Norm had the foresight and courage to invest in developing a condominium complex in Vail, Colorado, which was in its pioneering stage.

This proved to be a real boon to the three entrepreneurs who knew how to take calculated risks. Norm and Eunice enjoyed the ski slopes, and Vail was the result of their first meager sweat equity projects which commenced with the house they built in 1952.[2]

Turning Points

The rapid growth of the first branch at Wahpeton encouraged Bill and Norm to look elsewhere for additional opportunities. Two major events took place in the 1960s that assured continued growth. First, Grafton, which opened in 1963, developed at a slower pace than Wahpeton, but it was a solid community and helped to spread the Metropolitan name in the area. Second, during his monthly audit Norm noticed they had over $1 million in savings accounts from people with a Grand Forks mailing address. He learned that

that had come about because of a very active and influential board member from the area adjacent to Grand Forks. These people encouraged Metro to expand to "the Forks," as it was called locally. Another key factor was that the Holiday Inn in "the Forks" had borrowed $750,000 from the Fargo office and Metro made it appear that the loan was from Grafton.

Metro had applied to establish in Grand Forks but was turned down by the State Banking Board, which was made up of commercial bankers who were reluctant to allow any thrift to enter a community that they considered to have an adequate number of financial institutions. Attorney Mike Nilles represented the company as it presented its appeal to the State Banking Board, which was made up of four commercial bankers and one savings and loan manager. It was Nilles' task to show that there was a need for a thrift that Metro had failed to prove in its first attempt. In addition to the State Banking Board, the application drew opposition from Grand Forks' financial institutions and the North Dakota State Banks Association.

Norm pointed out that the Grafton branch already had $1 million in savings from Grand Forks residents, and it had loaned $750,000 in Grand Forks to the Holiday Inn, which was under construction. He continued that the Veteran's Administration (VA) was concerned because in the previous eleven months, it had made only twenty-three loans in the area while the VA in Fargo had made 248. Norm continued that the Fargo trade area, with a population of 117,000, had eighteen financial institutions while Grand Forks, with 91,500 people, had only nine banks. John Good, a loan guaranty officer for the VA, said that they were concerned about the lack of VA mortgage money in the area. But under cross examination he stated that except for Fargo and Grand Forks, all of North Dakota was considered a credit shortage area. The chief witness for the Grand Forks banks was John Cook, president of Valley Bank and a Nilles' brother-in-law, said that his bank had a good supply of money for loans, and since Metro was already loaning funds in the area, it had no reason for a branch office. However, Metro prevailed, and in August 1968 it opened its third branch in what had been the Dotty Dunn Hat Shop.

Shortly after that branch opened, Metro provided $6 million for purchase or construction of single family homes and $2.6 million to finance mobile homes. The opening of the Grand Forks branch was important because it was the second largest city in the state and a stepping stone to establishing branches in other communities. When the year ended, Metro was still the third-ranking thrift in the North Dakota Savings and Loan Association with 15.1 percent of the Association's assets behind Minot Federal with 16.1 percent and Gate City with 24.8 percent. The next highest association held 7.7 percent of the State Association's assets.

Norm was one of the original directors of the Fargo Housing Authority and through that duty became acquainted with M. Danny Wall, who was the assistant director of the Fargo Urban Renewal project. The major goal of the project was to clean up the entire riverfront area, remove Front Street, and build an approved dike along the Red River to Ninth Avenue South. Metro was the developer of the Park East Apartment Complex on Urban Renewal land. This was a low-risk project for the developer, but it gave the young team of Norm and Bill a chance to test their abilities for it was the largest project that Metro had encountered, and it prepared them for greater projects. The Fargo Urban Renewal Project made Norm aware of the potential Metro had in Fargo, while the agricultural revolution continued to take its toll on the smaller and less diversified communities of the state. Even more important, Wall was transferred to Washington, D.C., in 1972 where he became the director of the FHLB and FSLIC to oversee the federal savings and loan program.

Even though the company grew in assets every year, steadily rising expenses consistently plagued management. Mike Nilles related that the true test of leadership and a key to Metro's culture revealed itself one year when Bill and Norm volunteered to take a 4 percent reduction in their salaries so the lowest paid employees could have an increase.

Culture was maintained in other ways. Betty Ihry had taken a leave to accompany her husband in the military in Germany; she experienced a working environment far different from that at Metropolitan. She returned to work with the company as soon as her husband was released from the military and worked until she took maternity leave; then she was not sure that she wanted to return to work. Betty was a superb worker, so Bill Nilles called her several times and asked her to return. She was bored with typing

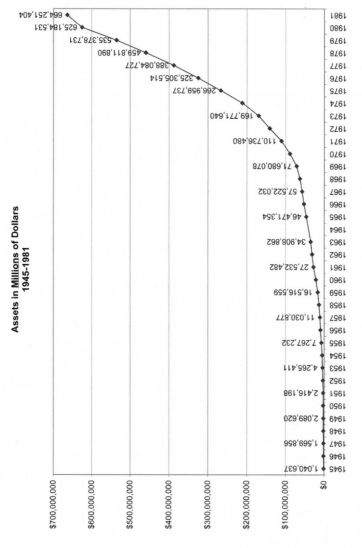

Assets in Millions of Dollars 1945-1981

Year	Value
1945	1,040,637
1946	1,569,856
1947	2,089,620
1949	2,416,198
1951	4,265,411
1953	7,267,232
1955	11,030,877
1957	16,516,559
1959	27,532,482
1961	34,908,862
1963	46,471,354
1965	57,522,032
1967	71,680,078
1969	110,736,480
1971	169,771,640
1973	266,959,737
1975	325,305,514
1976	388,084,727
1977	459,811,890
1978	535,378,731
1979	625,184,531
1980	664,251,404

Norm Jones became president in 1967 when Metro was in the take-off stage, at the same time the industry was confronting crisis. Compare this chart (in millions of dollars) with the one in chapter two, page 37 (in thousands), and the one in chapter six, page 173 (in billions).

87

loan papers and said she wanted to be a loan officer, so in 1973 she gained the distinction of being the first female to hold that position. She found the work much more exciting and very rewarding.

When Bob Clark graduated from college, he never looked elsewhere because he wanted to remain in the area. In 1975 he joined the Metro accounting department where most of its transactions were still done manually. He thoroughly enjoyed the work, but equally important he appreciated the family atmosphere clearly headed by Norm. Clark said Norm took pride in setting the tone and also in knowing everyone by first name. "I saw him every day and he always had something to say."

In 1970 the Metropolitan Service Corporation (MSC) had been created to manage other property not directly related to banking. Its primary purpose was to set up branch mortgage production offices built in Billings and Bozeman, Montana; Schaumberg, Illinois; Vail, Colorado; and Phoenix, Arizona. These communities all had active building programs where a higher rate of interest could be earned than in Fargo because North Dakota's usury law limited interest to a maximum of 12 percent. MSC also was used to finance new branch offices that were being leased or built. It also backed small-town governmental units to provide funds for low-cost housing projects.

By the close of 1976, the Association's assets had grown to $325 million, up from $25,000 in 1926; this represented a compounded growth rate of 20.86 percent per year for half a century. This represented the net growth after paying dividends most years, which totaled $7,374,000 in 1976 alone. At that time the Association had 57,000 savers and nearly 6,000 loans, mostly home mortgages of which 3,500 were with the Fargo office. Home loans generally were considered the least risky loans, partly because they were owner-occupied and regulations required strict lending practices.

In Metro's case, the major reasons for serious delinquencies on mortgage loans were: (1) a change in employment; (2) marital problems; and (3) alcoholism and subsequent inability to handle finances. The credit department in the Fargo office had a remarkable record. Each year started with eight to fifteen foreclosures in process, but by year's end only three or four were actually foreclosed; the rest were nurtured to a happier solution. This reflected good work by the loan underwriters who approved the loans and also of those who worked with the holders of delinquent mortgages to come to satisfactory results.

At this time Norm was on many civic boards in the Fargo Moorhead area in addition to serving two years as chair of the Fargo Housing Authority; past president of the North Dakota Savings and Loan League; director and vice-chairman of the Federal Home Loan Bank of the Des Moines district; and a member of the board and the executive committee for the Savings and Loan Computer Trust of Des Moines, one of the FHLB's largest savings and loan computer centers serving more than 200 institutions in the Midwest.[3]

More Branches and Continued Growth

After gaining experience in establishing the first three branches—Wahpeton, Grafton, and Grand Forks—Norm, with Bill to take care of the details, sensed the opportunities ahead. The 1970s was a good decade for agriculture, a major industry of the state, so Norm took advantage of the opportunity and set out to establish new branches in most of its viable communities. In September 1970 a branch was opened at Langdon, near the Canadian border, and Lisbon, in the southern Valley. Both were smaller communities than Grafton and Wahpeton but were still good business communities.

Metro was looking for a site near the new West Acres Mall because Norm was very excited about long-term potential for the area. However, he realized that they did not want to locate within the mall because historically those branches were not good money-makers. Norm contacted Bill Schlossman, the principal investor in the mall, who suggested a strip of land at its entrance. On August 23, 1972, Metro established branch number six adjacent to the West Acres Mall in a mobile home on a spacious opening strategically located at the entrance to the large shopping center. The temporary office was quickly moved to the space so the company could become the first financial institution in that area to capitalize on the heavy traffic flow and to get deposits from rural people who did not have easy access to a thrift or a bank in their community. The office opened with a staff of two who handled the traditional savings accounts and all types of loans with an emphasis on home loans.

An architect was instructed to design a unique, eye-catching, six-sided building to be occupied in May 1973. The attractive, wide-open space had the most land covered with "snow in the winter and the most grass to mow in the summer," but it was profitable from the start. Large United States and North Dakota flags were mounted on tall poles on the premises and, despite the considerable effort required to dismount them, both flags were stolen three times in the first four years. By 1977 a staff of eleven was needed to handle the business, which grew as the volume of traffic increased to the shopping center and Metro's services were altered to fit the customer demands. The growing and progressive mall area was noticed by the competition, and by 1977 three banks and two other S&Ls had joined the ranks of financial firms in West Acres.

On July 1, 1974, Clarence Bladow was transferred from his position as the manager of the Wahpeton branch to Fargo to become branch coordinator. At that time there were six branches, and plans were in process to seek out viable communities in North Dakota where Metro could establish new savings and loans. It was Bladow's responsibility to visit each branch monthly.

Bill Nilles said,

> Norm, with his personality, really developed first statewide and then national contacts that helped us make acquisitions. We had been conservative for so long that we had good reserves when so many associations were starting to get into trouble with their loans because of the changing rural economy, while we had better quality loans because of stable economy in Fargo.

Even though the agriculture economy was good in the 1970s, farm consolidation continued, which led to diminishing populations in nearly all agriculturally based counties, and rural towns experienced a reduction in business.

Norm read the association and federal publications about trends in the thrift industry. When he learned that a North Dakota thrift had a decline in deposits or was otherwise showing signs of trouble, he made it a point to contact the manager, who he usually knew through association activities. "I would call on the manager-president of those S&Ls and convince them that they could improve their position if they merged with us. We could not buy them. They were a mutual; they had to merge with us." This generally strengthened the ailing thrift and helped the local manager save face in the community. In this manner Metro was able to establish new thrifts or to acquire all of the existing thrifts in North Dakota with the exception of Gate City. By the 1980s Norm became nationally known in the industry, and when Metro expanded into other states, he was able to use the same technique with problem S&Ls.

After Metro had established or acquired a new branch, it was David Green's or Bev Austin's job to get the cooperation of the local merchants to conduct a community-wide promotion campaign. Initially, Norm had done the promotion work, but in the late 1960s he engaged an ad agency out of Chicago that was associated with the United States Savings and Loan League for guidance. Metro paid the newspaper advertising for the Metro Days campaign, which sometimes lasted up to a week. Each day a local merchant was featured and gave out prizes. To be eligible for the drawing, individuals had to register at Metropolitan's new office. Earlier Green had written jingles and some ads, but because of the rapid growth during the decade, he was given the job of planning Metro Days in the weeks after a new branch office was established.

In 1974 Metro opened three offices—Minot in April, Valley City in November, and Bismarck in December. After those three offices were opened, Metro was acknowledged as being the third-largest gainer among savings and loans in the nation with a 25.6 percent increase in deposits during a period when the industry experienced a 7.9 percent growth. Metro rose from 313th among S&Ls in 1973 to 254th in 1974.

In 1974 Wahpeton completed a new office, and the staff of fourteen conducted the dedication, which was held the last three days of two consecutive weeks. This produced over 10,000 registrations each week for door prizes, which included $1,500 in gift certificates per day and the coveted grand prize—a new Chevrolet Chevette.

In December 1975 an office was opened in Northwood, and during 1976, Lakota, New Rockford, Beach, and Dickinson all had new Metropolitan offices. They were followed by Mott, 1978; Williston, 1979; Rugby, 1980; and Harvey, 1981. Metro had established nineteen full-service offices in the state. It had become

Popular radio commentator Paul Harvey (left) visiting with Norm in the early 1970s. Harvey was sponsored by Metro from 1973 for the next two decades. His program proved to be very valuable.

the largest savings and loan in North Dakota with assets of nearly $650 million and reserves of over $24 million.

David Green, the major public relations person, saw his job change in 1975 when Maurice "Morrie" Jones Jr. with an MBA in marketing, joined the company. To enhance Metro's name recognition, Morrie engaged Myron Floren, the featured accordionist with the nationally-known Lawrence Welk orchestra, for a statewide television promotion campaign, "Live a Little Better with Metropolitan Federal." At each program Floren announced that the checks from his one-night engagements were deposited into his Metropolitan savings account. The popular radio personality, Paul Harvey, was sponsored for noon-day broadcasts and for speaking events in the area.

Customers who had deposits of at least $10,000 could become Metro Club members. Each branch has a special club room decorated in a Scandinavian motif, usually designed by Min Jones. Cookies, coffee, and other goodies were available, along with the *Wall Street Journal* and magazines. The Fargo club room contained a beautiful Bible given by Martin Jones' brother and wife. Members of the Metro Club who wanted to attend a performance by Floren in the state could arrange with the Club for transportation to the event. In essence, the Club became a travel service for its members with trips to the Twin Cities, Winnipeg, and elsewhere. It proved popular among seniors, who did not like using commercial agencies and were not comfortable driving.

The largest premium promotion campaign that the company staged came December 14, 1982, when the Metro Investment Account was introduced. Its purpose was to give the company an opportunity to be competitive with money market mutual funds. This campaign produced over 3,500 new accounts in thirty-three days. In January 1983 a "Big Ticket" premium campaign was initiated, and within six weeks 333 items were given, which brought in $4,549,382 in savings. By fall, 858 gift items had attracted $10,530,000 in deposits.

With one exception this was the last premium campaign. In June 1985 during the Scandinavian Hjemkomst Festival, Metro sponsored a Mini-Festival Special Offer. When new accounts were opened or loans were made, participants received discounted or free copies of *Hans Ola og Han Per*, a book based on the Norwegian-American comic strip co-edited by Concordia professor Joan Buckley. Over 1,000 copies were handed out that week. Norm stated that after Metro became a stock company, premiums were no longer offered. Some employees felt that savers watched for the premium programs and withdrew their funds to go to a competing S&L to open an account there, but Norm said that this happened in less than 5 percent of the cases. Once a customer started with Metro, they usually remained with them.[4]

Coping With Growth In The 1970s—Personal Experiences

Betty Ihry stated that the family atmosphere diminished in the 1970s when Metro started to grow so rapidly—the little impromptu parties became less frequent. "With every new merger the mortgage department was under real pressure, and it took many overtime hours to catch up with the work." But many labor saving devices were introduced that eased the work load, and she realized "that the good old days are now." In 1974 the automatic pay and deposit system, which enabled customers to automatically transfer funds between their accounts, was a real boon to the customer and a time saver for the tellers. In 1975 the Treasury Department and the Social Security Administration provided the opportunity for Social Security recipients to have their monthly payments electronically transferred direct to their accounts. At that time Metro had about 57,000 savings accounts. A large portion was with retirees.

After Eilene Sweet's three children were all enrolled in school, one day in late 1970 she saw an ad in the Lisbon paper for a part-time position as a second teller at the Metropolitan Savings and Loan, which had opened in September.

> I applied. I was not concerned about the pay—my first priority was just having something to do. Every day was exciting. My husband and I decided since we had always lived on his income we should save all of my income. We opened a savings account in 1970 and it is still there [2007].

In 1970 all the Lisbon office handled was saving accounts and certificates of deposits (CDs), but business grew rapidly, and in July 1972 Eilene became the second full-time teller. Some times she had to call Fargo for help. She said,

> I always felt so comfortable with Norman—he was so approachable and willing to answer. Bill [Nilles] was a little different—you had to think a little before you asked him. He was so sharp but all business. You could visit with Norman about anything.

In August 1976 the manager, Larry Hanna, was promoted to loan manager at Grand Forks, and Eilene became Metro's first female branch manager.

In 1982 S&Ls were permitted to offer checking accounts. That was a "big and exciting change, as was every new product introduction," because every new product had the potential to greatly increase the volume of daily customers. As manager, Eilene took applications for loans, made the appraisal, and did the credit report and the paper work. Sometimes couples applied for loans. They both worked but had no savings and had no idea where they spent their money. She worked with many such clients and eventually was able to finance them. When she retired in 1995, not a single loan that she had approved had gone into default in her two decades of making loans.

In his first job after graduating from college, Gary Dietz got a job with a thrift. He quickly discovered that he did not like the company culture for it operated solely for its own good, so he left. He let a friend in Metro know that he would like to work for the company, and in early 1971 he got a call from Norm and was hired as branch manager in Grand Forks. Shortly after he became manager he called Norm because an elderly person came in with an outdated passbook account which included a refundable coupon with interest. Norm advised him to honor it and treat it as a current regular passbook account and to do the same with other outdated investments. This included redeeming the Class "H" Installment Shares purchased during 1930-32. Dietz observed first hand that everything he had heard about the integrity of Maurice, Norm, and Metro was true.

In April 1971 the Grand Forks office was still located in the Dotty Dunn Hat Shop building that it first rented in August 1968. The business had grown rapidly to $100 million in deposits, and it was time for larger quarters. On October 4, 1972, ground was broken on DeMers Avenue for a five-story building at a projected cost of $1.1 million. Metro Days were held October 29 through November 9, 1973, during which time the $1.3-million building was dedicated. The *Grand Forks Herald* devoted fourteen pages to the event. Dietz recalled that the Grand Forks branch was very competitive with interest rates and was able to generate deposits, but local investment opportunities were not readily available.

At the final 1975 board meeting, an executive committee was established consisting of Norm Jones, Bill Nilles, Tony Renner, Clarence Bladow, Gary Dietz, and Dave Einerson. Its responsibility was to meet twice monthly to discuss policies and procedures to handle the larger work load. The timing was great, for in the next four years Metro's assets grew from $300 million to $625 million.

Metro's reputation as *the* place to work became apparent when 120 applications were received to establish a Human Resource Department. In 1976 David Lysne became the first director. He observed the culture was great, for employees still had the freedom to make mistakes. Up to that time employing was done by department heads and employee records were still done by hand. Lysne's first task was to formalize the hiring process, payroll records, and job descriptions. This was the period when federal mandates about employment procedures were being inaugurated and great changes were being made.

The Joneses had always been very careful about employing people, but they were more careful about discharging. Lysne did all preliminary screening of applicants and selected two or three for the department supervisors. No matter how careful the interviewing process, the unpleasant task of having to ask a few to leave remained, but sometimes "it was satisfying to learn that many did well later. We were not always the perfect fit or they had gained something in the process of being let out."

Bob Clark's first job was doing payroll, and when finished with that, he did general accounting. He manually prepared 130 checks for each pay period. "There were a few computers but they were only for specific tasks." Little did he realize how quickly conditions would change. In 1980 Norm returned from the regional FHLB meeting in Des Moines where he had observed that computers could be programmed to do many more tasks. He quickly sensed the labor-saving advantages of using more computers. He called a meeting of the accounting department and asked who wanted to try computer programming. Clark, who had taken a few computer courses in college, recalled, "My arm shot up and I became their first computer programmer." Metro was on the system with Des Moines, which did the customer data primarily for collecting the daily teller programs.

For his first eighteen months, Clark was the only programmer, and most of the in-house functions were still done by hand. Because payroll was his primary task, he immediately computerized that job. One by one his colleagues came to him with their job, and Clark adapted it to the computer. In 1983 when Metro became a stock company, other programmers joined Clark to handle the broadening of regulations along with the new services that savings and loan institutions could offer. Clark stated that introducing checking accounts opened a whole set of problems that had not been a concern in the days of being just a thrift business. Overdrawn accounts, stop payment, insufficient accounts, and mailing statements to customers were new experiences and greatly increased the work load.

In August 1979 Rodney Jordahl was employed as an external auditor. His job was to visit each of the sixteen branches periodically. These visits varied from one to three days. In 1982 he was promoted to head of the auditing department just before the association made its largest coup to date when First Federal of Jamestown, Grand Forks Federal, and Northwest Federal of Williston and their combined thirty-four branches merged with Metro. Norm commented about that big move:

> Those three had $86 million, $84 million, and $118 million in assets respectively. I knew they were not doing well. I knew from reading annual federal publications that they were not growing like they had in the past and their resources were going down.

Those mergers gave Metro twenty-two locations in the state and increased its net assets to $1.032 billion. Jordahl added that Metro survived the early 1980s because it had always kept its reserves strong and had avoided making risky loans when many others were tempted to do so. But the family environment changed when deregulation made the industry much more competitive.

On the thirtieth anniversary of Norm's service to Metro, director Ray Whiting wrote: "Norm's ability to learn and to compete as the rules have changed [has kept the association in the forefront]. Norman is what I call an aggressive conservative. He makes things happen but always with a feel for the soundness of the transaction." Director Tryhus commented that Norm was not really challenged until deregulation came. "Then he got excited about what was ahead—almost as if he had a vision about it. That was a real turning point for him."[5]

A Period of Transition

According to Gary Dietz,

> The Jones philosophy penetrated Metropolitan all the way from top to bottom. We called it family, but today everyone calls it corporate culture. The good part of that was that there were very few misfits. There was a discipline at work and even at company parties. It was not spoken, but expected.

The Joneses were religious people, and they all confronted issues from an ethical standpoint. In the early days Martin and Maurice knew many of the people they employed and were careful to protect their reputation. The Fargo population was less diverse than it is today, and it was easier to maintain the culture when most of the employees fit the mold.

Maurice Sr. was good at sensing what appealed to the customers—for example, the Johnny Appleseed Club, step-stools so the very young could make deposits and then select a lollypop, a Metro Club with a room for coffee and cookies and the *Wall Street Journal*. The larger branches even had hostesses who wrapped premium gifts and organized tours. His people skills were superb. His laid-back, country style made people comfortable with him, and "he was an advisor to everybody." A friend, who was not a customer, commented that Maurice had piqued his interest in farming and "steered me to a section of land." David Green had no intention of buying a place at the lake, "but Maurice wanted us to have one, and guess where we landed? Norm, who was very good at architecture, drew a plan for our cabin; it was very good."

Noel Fedje recalled that after it became known that Maurice was suffering from cancer, he went fishing by himself and fell into the lake while trying to get the motor started. It did not start. Later, after he was rescued, Maurice commented that he had to stay afloat or "some would think that I had committed suicide."

Nancy Kegel grew up on a farm in northern Montana. She was very talented musically and was set on going to Concordia College, where she relied on scholarships, loans, and a job to make her way. She apparently was not bashful, for on her third night on campus she met Morrie Jones at a dance. From that day on she felt like a member of the Jones family. Nancy and Morrie dated through the first three years of college. "He loved people and people loved him—a fun person to be with."

Except for one summer while in college, Morrie worked at Metropolitan. Norm wanted him to work for the company, but neither he nor Morrie felt totally comfortable about his working there. Maurice's cancer was progressing rapidly, so Morrie and Nancy decided to marry after their junior year and would do so in Fargo because Maurice would not be able to go to Montana.

Maurice Jones Jr. (Morrie), 1950-1987. Morrie joined Metro in 1975 as its first professionally trained marketing specialist. His program greatly increased the company's recognition.

Three weeks before the date of the wedding, Morrie and Nancy were out of state and were called home. "He died a few moments after we got to his bedside [May 15, 1971]. He was waiting." Nancy and Morrie were married as planned and in their senior year at college they lived in an apartment where Nancy worked as resident manager and Morrie worked at a pizza place.

In 1972 after graduating from Concordia with a degree in business, Morrie entered the University of Minnesota to work toward an MBA. Nancy taught elementary school music in north Minneapolis. In 1975 after earning his MBA, Morrie sought other jobs because he had no interest in returning to Fargo. David

Green said, "He wanted to be his own person, but in the end he joined Metro—the family loyalty was so strong." Nancy said, "We prayed about where to go and the message was clear that we should go to Fargo." Bill Nilles recalled, "Norm knew that he could not convince him [Morrie] to come to Metro so he asked me to talk to him. My job was to get him to give Metro a try. Norm said, 'Go to $12,000 with him,' but I had to go to $13,000. Maurice Jr. was really skilled when it came to marketing."

Morrie joined the company as an assistant vice president and head of the marketing department. Unlike Norm, who had worked at all jobs in the company, Morrie's first task was to start the marketing program. It was what he had prepared for. Nancy commented, "He was always sure to do more than his share because he was a Jones and did not want to be accused of shirking." It was not long before Norm and Morrie were working as a team and everyone felt like family. Dorothy Kellerman, who worked under Morrie, said he was just like the other Joneses, "so down-to-earth and they all made you feel so good. You just wanted to work for them." Just like the two generations preceding him, Morrie was soon immersed in a wide range of community activities, and by 1978, only three years after returning to Fargo, he was holding office in six different organizations.

The 1970s and early 1980s were exciting years at Metro because of the rapid rate of establishing new offices and then making mergers. Mike Nilles commented that Norm had the ability to sense a good merger project and, in the words of one of his executive committee, "would go for it a hundred miles per hour. On the other hand, Morrie was not as deliberate as Bill Nilles but would at least seek for the unknowns before acting." Mike Nilles added, "Morrie prepared the applications to the national board very thoroughly for every institution Metro sought to acquire. The bureaucrats were overwhelmed with the data that was presented and we got all but one that we applied for. Hillsboro was the only one we lost because Grand Forks Federal got their papers in first. Excitement filled the air." Nancy recalled that she never saw Morrie stressed at work. He always got up and went to work with enthusiasm. He so liked his work. He had a good balance of work, but he played hard too. He worried about friends at work who did not have that balance."[6]

A New Venture For Min

In August 1972 Min, who for the first 46 years of her marriage was a happy, busy, stay-at-home mother, opened the Stabo Scandinavian Imports shop in the West Acres Mall. This new life proved to be a real boon. She said, "I kept very busy at the shop and I never felt tired because I so enjoyed it." Like the men in the family, she enjoyed meeting people and knew how to sell. Up to this time, besides giving strong moral support to her husband and sons, her major contribution to the company had been designing the Metro Club rooms. That culminated in establishing the Toly Dager Julefest (Twelve Days of Christmas), which became an annual event in all of Metropolitan's North Dakota offices. But her new life was more than the Stabo, for she became more active in civic and church activities and served as president of several organizations in the community. Her crowning achievement in these activities was being co-chair of one of the most successful community projects, a 462-page First Lutheran Church cookbook, which went through five editions in nine years. Her community involvement led to her being chosen as the 1980 YWCA Fargo-Moorhead Businesswoman of The Year. The Stabo continued to thrive under her management, but at age seventy-five she decided to retire so she could spoil her grandchildren.

Nancy, the fourth woman to enter the family, had one thing in common with Birgit, Min, and Eunice—they all grew up on farms and had few worldly possessions. Twenty years after the death of Morrie, Nancy commented about her experience with the Jones family, especially with Min:

> I learned so much by watching Min. It was a tremendous learning opportunity. My first impression was in awe of her self-confidence, social graces, and zest for life. I think back how God made things happen in her life. The focus she had for life, for guiding others, even what she read. She was so much strength to me. She loved me like a daughter. The last time I was with her I had my accordion and played and sang hymns for her.[7]

Problems In The Thrift Industry

In the 1950s and 1960s the housing industry created a boom for the thrift industry, which operated under protective regulations and in an economy with stable interest rates until 1966. Then, interest rates rose and inflation made conditions more unstable. The North Dakota usury law placed a ceiling on interest rates on deposits the S&Ls could pay, which was lower than the market rate. Savers transferred their funds to where they could receive higher earnings. This created a shortage of funds for home construction and slowed economic expansion. The same regulations that previously had helped the industry led to stagnation in the late 1970s.

By April 1977 Metro had grown to a membership in excess of 67,000 with assets of $388 million. Then, two changes were made in regulations that helped the industry. In 1979 a four-year treasury certificate was introduced with a monthly variable interest rate, and assets exceeded $535 million. In 1980 a checking account paying 5.25 percent interest compounded daily was available and assets reached $625 million. In 1980 Norm finally achieved one of the family's long-sought goals. Metro added $1.5 million to its reserves for a total of $23.7 million and finally passed Gate City.

While many S&Ls were falling on hard times because of risky investments and sometimes questionable practices, Metro continued on Martin Jones' course of financing home loans and other low-risk financial opportunities. In 1981 the company had an increase in savings of $481 million. It was a year of innovation for the industry: the adjustable rate loan; the All Savers Certificate, which made the first $2,000 income on savings accounts exempt from federal taxes; the Individual Retirement Account (IRA) allowed wage earners covered by pension plans to open a savings account and shelter both the deposit and interest from federal income tax. Ironically, because of rapidly rising expenses, 1981 was the only year in the Association's history that it had an operating loss.

By 1980 the industry was losing money for the first time since the '30s, and the problem accelerated when the rate of new home construction fell to a thirty-five-year low. From 1980 to

1982, a total of 843 S&Ls disappeared. In 1981 and '82 the industry lost $11.6 billion and was facing an industry-wide threat of insolvency. To save themselves, many failing thrifts sought to be acquired by another. Thrifts with a high net worth but saddled with excessive operating costs or those unable to attract new capital were targets for acquisition, but the mergers avoided the scrutiny of the supervisory agencies.

In 1982 Congress passed legislation that deregulated the financial services industry, and the S&Ls were able to make commercial loans and offer an array of other financial services. Interest rates were reduced, and the thrift industry increased its assets to $691 billion up from $602 billion in 1980. This appeared to be a boon, but the industry was not growing at the same rate as the economy. Metropolitan, with Bill, Morrie, and Norm at the helm, was destined to make its mark on the entire industry. Supervisory mergers were initiated by FSLIC or the FDIC by compelling the failing firms to make managerial changes so they would be able to survive.

Norm, who was serving on national boards, saw that the future was with a stock company and a federal charter. He sensed the opportunity that was open for Metro. To take advantage of what was ahead, Metro switched from being a state chartered mutual company to a federally chartered mutual. The name was changed to Metropolitan Federal Savings and Loan. Norm commented, "This had a psychic affect." The second reason for the change was that North Dakota law did not allow a stock chartered savings and loan, and the federal did. Nationwide, many S&Ls were converting this way because it was the best way to raise capital to build strong reserves. Mutual firms had difficulty building reserves because they had to compete on paying dividends. By becoming a stock company, Metro was free to use the market to raise money to continue making acquisitions.

In any case, no time was lost converting to a stock company. On December 29, 1982, Norman M. Jones sent a lengthy and very detailed letter to all Metropolitan members. It stated that the FHLBB agreed that the Metropolitan Federal Savings and Loan Association of Fargo could be converted from a federally chartered mutual association to a federally chartered capital stock association. The letter was sent with a proxy form to be returned for those who could not attend the meeting on February 3, 1983, for the purpose of considering the conversion. It explained that saving and borrowing members would lose voting rights, which would fall to the domain of the stockholders unless they purchased stock in the new company. But Norm emphasized that all deposits were still protected by the FSLIC.

Norm's letter stated that the S&Ls had to compete with other financial institutions for funds. This caused a sharp increase in cost of funds for the entire industry. At the same time, the savings outflow continued, which diminished the growth of savings and adversely affected the lending ability because fewer funds were available. Congress reacted and on October 15, 1982, passed the Garn-St. Germain Deposit Institutions Act, which changed the way the S&L industry could do business. Federally chartered S&Ls were authorized to make commercial, agricultural, and corporate loans up to 5 percent of their assets, and after January 1, 1984, up to 10 percent. The act also permitted money market deposit accounts for banks and S&Ls to be competitive with money market mutual funds. A clause that later proved very important to Metro stated that the FHLBB was granted authority to approve interstate and inter-industry mergers, subject to bidding procedures. Norm added that in addition to increasing the cost of funds, the act would increase competition with banks. Norm emphasized, "The long-range effect of this legislation on the overall economic situation of the savings and loan industry cannot be predicted at this time." At that time no one could have imagined that within a decade Norm would become a major person in the industry in the Midwest.

At the time Metro had 339 employees, of which thirty-three were on a part-time basis. In addition to the home office in Fargo, it had thirty-four branch offices throughout North Dakota. Mortgage loans were also made from offices in Denver and Vail, Colorado, and Scottsdale, Arizona, from which they also made construction loans to builders in those areas. It also had Metropolitan Service Corporation, a wholly-owned subsidiary.

Norm emphasized that after 1980, regulations permitted broader lending activities. Metropolitan "continued on a conservative program of concentrating on conventional first mortgage loans for the construction or purchase of one- to four-unit residential properties." Its loan portfolio on such properties made up 84.1 percent of total assets. The remainder of the loans consisted of first mortgages on commercial property, larger than four-unit residential property, government securities, second mortgages on residential property, plus mobile homes, improvement loans, and savings-account-secured loans. Most of its loans were made at or below the 80 percent appraisal limitation.

In addition to all of above, the letter contained financial figures indicating how the Association had grown and strengthened in recent years. Because of the rapid growth, it was determined that Metro should become a stock company. Norm envisioned what was ahead and was thrilled to have Morrie involved with the conversion and mergers from the start. Morrie handled all the publications and was on hand for "what became the largest expansion of a retail banking operation in the Midwestern United States."[8]

~ ~ ~ ~ ~

1. A tabulation of company assets in Jones files; a typed biography of Norman Jones in files; Tryhus interview; Golberg interview; Fedje interview Norman Jones interview.

2. Tryhus interview; typed biography of Bill Nilles in files; Mike Nilles interview; interview of Gary Dietz, Fargo, March 13, 2007, hereafter Dietz interview; Kvamme interview; interview of David Lysne, Fargo, April, 30, 2007, hereafter Lysne interview; Bill Nilles interview.

3. Norman Jones interview; Mike Nilles interview; *Bismarck Tribune*, January 8, 1968; Record of the North Dakota Savings and Loan Association's assets 1967 to 1984; Kvamme interview; Dietz interview; Green interview; Bill Nilles interview; Tryhus interview; interview of Bob Clark, Fargo, April 25, 2007, hereafter Clark interview; Renner interview; Binford; *Metro Line*, page 4, August 1976, a company newsletter, hereafter *Metro Line*.

4. Fedje interview; *Grand Forks Herald*, October 28, 1968; Bill Nilles interview; Norman Jones interview; Bladow interview; Green interview; *Minot Daily News*, June 22, 1974; *Valley City Times-Record*, November 19, 1974; *Metro Line*, December 1974, March 1975, August 1976, December 1977, August 1979, April, September-December 1982, March, September 1983.

5. Ihry interview; *Metro History*, pp. 11-12; interview of Eilene Sweet, Fargo, April 23, 2007, hereafter Sweet interview; *Metro Line* August 1976, September 1979, July 1982; Dietz interview; *Grand Forks Herald*, October 28, 1973; Clark interview; Lysne interview; interview of Rodney Jordahl, Fargo, March 7, 2007, hereafter Jordahl interview; Tryhus interview; Norman Jones interview.

6. Dietz interview; Golberg interview; Fedje interview; Schafer interview; *Montana Agriculture Basic Facts*, Bulletin 664, Montana Agricultural

Experiment Station and Cooperative Extension Series, (Bozeman, August 1973); Bill Nilles interview; Green interview; Skurdahl-Jones, p. 76; Kellerman iinterview; Mike Nilles interview.

7. Binford, pp. 24, 27, 34-35; Schafer interview; telephone interview of Harriet Ritter Mauritsen, Chino Valley, Arizona, June 27, 2008, hereafter Mauritsen interview; interview of John Pierce, Moorhead, Minnesota, June 27, 2008, hereafter Pierce interview.

8. Andrew S. Carron, *The Rescue of the Thrift Industry: Studies in the Regulation of Economic Activity* (Washington, D.C.: The Brookings Institution, 1983), pp. VII, 2,4-5, 7, 12; Andres S. Carron, *The Plight of the Thrift Institutions* (Washington, D.C.: The Brookings Institution, 1982), pp. VII, 1, 5, 7; Norman Jones interview; Norman Jones, letter to members, December 29, 1982, hereafter Jones letter; Skurdall-Jones, p. 101.

Chapter V

From Fargo to Wall Street
1983-1988

A Troubled Industry In Retrospect

During the 1980s another 525 thrift institutions were liquidated or sold at an estimated cost to the FSLIC of $47 billion. When the decade came to an end, another eighteen were ready to be acquired or merged, which would add another $7 billion to the cost. In addition, there were 517 insolvent firms still operating, waiting to be liquidated at a potential cost of $100 billion. When the 1990s started, another thousand firms were struggling to survive. James R. Barth, author of *The Great Savings and Loan Debacle*, blamed the FSLIC for failing to achieve its goal. The government underestimated the problem, so its following actions made the situation worse.

Many thrifts were insolvent before deregulation took place, but the problem was slightly intensified by some S&L managers who practiced risky activities when the industry was deregulated; some even looted their institutions. The real culprit was that at the advent of the 1980s, the industry was primarily invested in fixed-rate residential mortgages and was funded by deposits that received a higher rate of interest. The chief reason was that the government had provided tax incentives to fund home purchases and prohibited the S&Ls from deliberately diversifying their portfolios; in addition, they were also not allowed to offer adjustable-rate loans until the 1980s.

In an attempt to minimize the impact on the public, the government reduced the capital requirements, loosened regulatory standards, changed the federal tax code to benefit the struggling institutions, and mergers were arranged to eliminate those thrifts

Mike Nilles, Metro's only in-house attorney, from 1984 to 1994.

that were insolvent by creating an asset called "goodwill" that was reported as regulatory capital. The goodwill asset was intended to delay the problem, which would disappear when interest rates came down. But the government did not impose sufficient regulations to restrain S&Ls from taking excessive risks; some were even fraudulent. This only intensified the problem.

The government wanted the S&Ls to provide service that other financial institutions were not providing, but because of state and then federal intrusion, the industry steadily became more inflexible and was not able to cope with the changing market forces. Barth commented, "We need reform with longer-term focus . . . a system in which the private sector's quest for profits is kept in check by its aversion to losses, thus more adequately protecting taxpayers."

Gary Dietz, a member of Metropolitan's management committee, reminisced that during the 1960s and after many S&Ls opened because there were few restrictions. Many of these firms were small and lacked sound management practices. When interest rates climbed, the regulators wanted to help them, and many wanted to link with stronger firms like Metro rather than go out of business. Fortunately, Norm was well respected in the industry and "was well wired in Washington and the leaders of the ailing firms were eager for a merger or buyer."

Mike Nilles seconded much of what was stated above and added that the regulators were a major cause of the S&L crisis "because they looked at assets [versus] liabilities rather than cash flow." The problem was compounded with the "inflation caused by the Vietnam War and the government printing more money." Then, the guidelines were loosened and the S&Ls did not know how to handle commercial lines after just working with the less risky home loans.[1]

Forming a Stock Company

Metro was not completely able to escape the problems that the thrift industry was experiencing and, as stated in the previous chapter, in 1981 had its first operating loss. After state and federal tax credits, the loss was $3.5 million. It recovered in 1982 and had a net income of $1.3 million. Total assets increased from $753.2 million in 1981 to $1.022 billion in 1982. Because of the conservative management style that the Jones family had always practiced, Metro had $22 million in reserves.

Norm had a grasp of the broad picture and in 1982 he used that knowledge to acquire three of the largest mutual associations in North Dakota—First Federal of Jamestown, Grand Forks Federal, and Northwestern Federal of Williston. Those associations had a combined total of thirty-four branch offices, 6,983 real estate loans, 54,664 savings accounts, assets of $286,019,751, and acquired goodwill of $44,932,248. All this was accomplished without any financial assistance from the FSLIC. On December 31, 1982, Metropolitan had 373 full-time employees, 45 part-time, and 28 at the Metropolitan Service Mortgage Corporation. Metro ended the year with assets of over $1 billion, deposits of $758 million, and retained income of $25 million. It had become the largest S&L in North Dakota and one of only two that survived the 1980s. The other was its friendly competitor, Gate City. Metro ranked 124 out of 2,426 in the nation. Everyone was very upbeat when 1982 ended because of the great rebound that Metro had experienced while much of the rest of the industry was suffering. Rod Jordahl, who worked on acquisitions, commented that the board trusted in the abilities of Morrie and Norm as leaders and was ready to go public.

In retrospect Norm said,

> We had a big year in 1982 when we went from a state charter [mutual] to a federal charter, which permitted us to become a stock company. Under a state charter we could not go into other states and we could not become a publicly owned company.

The prospectus stated that the company served customers from western Minnesota, northern South Dakota, eastern Montana, and all of North Dakota. "We are ready to respond to opportunities for geographic expansion as a major regional savings and loan institution."

The prospectus also stated that since deregulation of the financial services industry, Metro had begun to expand its commercial loan activities and planned to add other types of financial services to enhance the long-term growth of stockholder equity. Metro already had six subsidiaries that were engaged in mortgage banking, real estate development, and sales. The mortgage bank offices were located in Denver and Vail, Colorado; Scottsdale, Arizona; and Palm Desert, California. It was not stated in the prospectus, but the interest rates were higher in those states than in North Dakota, and the demand for investment money in North Dakota was not sufficient to take all that Metro had available.

While the above activity was taking place, Norm was thinking ahead to the next step. Noel Fedje, manager of the local brokerage firm Dain Bosworth and a friend of Norm's in the "Norwegian legion" at First Lutheran, recalled that before he came to Fargo he had learned from Henry Norton, an expert on the thrift industry, how much money had been made on thrift stock. In a visit with Norm, Fedje recalled what Norton had told him about the money that investors had made on thrift stock by going public. Fedje continued:

> I recall visiting about it in our brokerage office and they downplayed it. Later, I was on vacation and I got a call from

Bob Ward, my assistant. Norm had been on Wall Street and got lots of encouragement. Then, the Dain people got excited. Norm had visited with David Saphio, of Salomon Brothers' Inc., one of the biggest firms on The Street. When Norm asked him if Metro should go public, he replied, 'We'll take you.' Morrie initially had some questions about going public and was particularly concerned about using larger national firms. Norm asked me [Fedje] to have a session with him and explain the risks and advantages. After that, Morrie was comfortable with the idea.

Norm explained in the prospectus that S&Ls were allowed to operate money market accounts, which enabled them to compete with money market mutual funds. He also explained capital assistance; the FSLIC was empowered to provide capital assistance using net worth certificates (mentioned earlier as "goodwill") to qualified associations that had incurred operating losses. The initial level of help could range up to 70 percent of such losses. The statutory reserve requirement was deleted, and the reserve and net worth levels were at the discretion of the FHLBB. Another change in the regulations authorized the FHLBB up to three years to approve intrastate and inter-industry mergers, subject to bidding procedures giving priority to mergers between institutions of the same type located within the same state.

Those changes were followed by permitting the super NOW account—a $2,500-minimum-balance account with no minimum maturity or maximum interest rate limitations and unlimited check writing privileges. The NOW account increased the cost of funds for S&Ls but enabled them to better compete with other investments during times of high interest rates. It also gave them more investment powers so they could be more competitive with other institutions. Norm apparently had some reservations on this point for he wrote, "The long-range effect of this legislation on the overall economic situation of the savings and loan industry cannot be predicted at this time."

In typical Jones concern for the customer/shareholder, Norm estimated that the net $20 million from the sale of stock would be invested in real estate loans and invested as permitted by putting funds into statutory reserved and net worth requirements. The balance would be placed into savings growth, more mortgage lending, relocating and expanding existing facilities, and establishment of additional branch offices. Once again he assured the customers that cash dividends would be paid on common stock.

After getting approval to become a stock company, meetings had to be held to let insiders have first opportunity to buy. The law required that Metro customers, either those with savings accounts or borrowers, employees, and management be given ninety days to purchase stock before it became available to the general public. Morrie plunged into the task of organizing the stock sale campaign, sometimes referred to as "dog and pony shows," and did most of the programming for the presentations to the insiders. Then, Norm, Morrie, and R.C. Crockett, a past executive secretary of the Greater North Dakota Association who was well known throughout North Dakota, went on the road to explain to the customers the opportunity they had to buy company stock. In the ninety days before going public, they made eleven presentations in the communities where Metropolitan was well established and best known. Norm said that he was told by the brokerage people that this was one of the most successful pre–sales campaigns they had ever experienced; all customers, officers, and employees bought stock. This was probably because of the very favorable reputation the Jones family had developed and the pro-customer stance Metro had taken in its operations. This made many first-time stock buyers comfortable with Metro stock.

Board member Doug Larsen recalled that many buyers had never owned stock before because they had always saved in fixed-rate investments, but "they bought because of their faith in the Joneses." Larsen needed the money his business generated to be put back into his business, but he felt so strongly about the stock that he borrowed a considerable sum to buy. He added, "A thousand dollars of stock purchased at the Initial Public Offering (IPO) left for dividend reinvestment was worth $50,000 at the end of the first quarter of 2007."

An employee pleaded with his father, who had never purchased stock, to buy Metropolitan. He reluctantly purchased 100 shares at the IPO for $1,175, and in July 1998 cashed them in for $60,000. A prominent Fargo businessman stated that he purchased a block of shares at the IPO and whenever he had extra money from that point on because "I knew their culture. Norm was on track and stretching out." Or, as Bill Bartkowshi commented, "Norm exuded boundless enthusiasm, which helped the cause."

Metro customers purchased 447,272 shares. Officers, directors, and employees bought another 219,498, which was 33 percent of the total offering. Norm was pleased with the results of the pre-sale because the family did not want distant owners and hoped that there would be many local buyers. Gary Dietz recalled that when Metro went public, Norm cautioned "all of us not to oversell the stock to people who were not risk-oriented. Later, when the stock became available to the general public, some employees sold their stock because they were not comfortable with owning stock."

The remaining stock went to forty-six brokerage firms, of which Salomon Brothers and Dain Bosworth took the largest blocks. Noel Fedje recalled that interest rates were very high on March 31, 1983, the day of the IPO, and some of the eastern firms did not seem too interested in the stock, so Dain Bosworth announced that they would take "all the stock any firm did not want because we could place it." Dain did so was because his firm's management had such tremendous faith in the Jones family and their analyst trusted Norm's management style. The IPO was successful, and 2,133,323 shares were sold, netting $22,847,000, which increased the net worth from $25 million to $48 million. This gave Norm the reserves he needed to pursue his vision. The September 19, 1983, *Fortune Magazine* article entitled "What are Some of the S&Ls You Find Attractive?" listed Metropolitan Federal as one of nine featured S&Ls, a good indication that Metro was moving to the front of the line of surviving thrifts.

The Chairman's Letter in the *1983 Annual Report* opened:

Dear Shareholder: Nineteen eighty-three was a year of significant growth for Metropolitan Federal in virtually every important respect. The year marked . . . the initiation of a formal strategic planning process that will set the course for the remainder of the 1980s.

With that introduction the report continued that while the slump of 1980-82 seriously affected most of the thrift industry, by late 1982 Metro had experienced a turnaround and recovered dramatically in 1983. In 1982, net interest earnings, after

The cover of the first annual report of the newly organized stock company, Metropolitan Federal Corporation.

provisions for losses of 1981, were $3.9 million and increased to $20 million in 1983. Net income had risen from $1.3 million to $8.2 million in those years. The reasons for the growth were: (1) Lower interest rates reduced the cost of funds and increased lending activity—Metro was able to profit from the sale of loans and mortgage-backed securities, and the proceeds were reinvested in the company service area to provide capital for customer needs; (2) The expanded deposit base from the acquisition of the Grand Forks, Jamestown, and Williston S&Ls and increased equity from the sale of stock by converting to a publicly owned association; (3) Mortgage lending and service activities increased in the fast-growing southwest sector of the country where Metro had three offices; (4) Adjustable rate mortgage (ARM) was well received in the Midwest, and loan demand was good in North Dakota, the company's primary service area. Loans originated and purchased in 1982 increased from $141 million to $326 million in 1983. At the same time, new deposits, exclusive of acquisition and mergers, rose from $17 million to $92 million.

A Strategic Planning Program was established to cope with the newly deregulated financial services industry. The basic mission was to continue offering savings and housing-related financial services to the upper Midwest while diversifying to offset the fluctuations in the interest rate cycles. Commercial lending serving the business and agricultural communities, plus commercial checking, were added to customer services, but further deregulation permitted more expansion into new functional areas. Rod Jordahl, who had become controller, commented that auditing was greatly altered because everything was open to the public. Much more of the activity had to be disclosed. The corporate function really changed—issuing stock and deciding to buy banks took so much time.

The cover page of the June 1984 *Metro Line* read: "Metropolitan Shares to Become Part of New NASDAQ National Market System NMS." Norm explained the advantages of being on the national market and closed by giving his reasons for going with NASDAQ. "Since NMS is considered by many to be the prime market for emerging blue chips, we believe that inclusion in the new system offers substantial benefits to Metropolitan Federal and to its shareholders."[2]

A Unique Management Team

It is unusual for three generations in one family to have similar traits that made them such good people persons, good managers of business, and so well liked by those who worked with them and the public in general. In 1981 Bill Bartkowski met Morrie at Toastmasters and they soon developed strong ties. In the early spring of 1984 he received a call from Morrie inquiring if he knew anything about investor relations. In April Bartkowski interviewed for such a position but could not "get [him]self to take it." Bartkowski had a master's degree in Theology and a PhD in Adult Education and was employed by the Catholic Diocese of Fargo. He went to the bishop, who suggested that he take the offer. A couple months later he was asked about any difference between working at the Diocese and at Metro. He replied, "Metropolitan has less politics and more Christians." Later, he added that Norm, a Republican and a devout Lutheran, was an interesting person. "He always liked to have Catholics and Democrats around." Bartkowski got personal satisfaction by that comment because he was a Catholic and a Democrat, but he was referring to the Nilles family, who were Catholics and Democrats and had been active in Metropolitan from the beginning.

Bartkowski was made Director of Corporate Communications under Morrie and was very involved in speaking for Metro. Bartkowski said he was amazed at how Norm conducted himself with everyone he met. He recalled that Norm was speaking somewhere in the South and he was asked what state was north of North Dakota. Norm hesitated and then politely said, "Canada." After the speech he told Bartkowski, "Maybe we should put Canada on the map so that would not embarrass others by asking the same question." Bartkowski stated that in his travels industry people, especially analysts, would ask, "Is Norm always that polite?

Board members and top level management recalled that they never heard Norm say no. If a suggestion was made and he was not sure he liked it, he would reply, "Let's think about it." If he liked the idea, he would reply, "Why aren't we doing it?" Bartkowski commented about a meeting of stock analysts that took place in 1988 when an analyst from Fidelity Fund, which had 9.9 percent of Metro's stock, asked Norm where he was going

Each member of the Thrift Institutions Advisory Council was given
a leather-bound folder with this seal embossed on the cover.

to move next. Norm replied, "To the contiguous states." Then the
questioner said, "You ought to go Tennessee because Saturn is
going to build there." Norm responded, "We'll have to think about
it." Those working closest to him understood immediately that he
was not interested.

After acquiring all the troubled thrifts available in North
Dakota, Norm had to look for new avenues to continue growing. In
1983, after realizing $23 million in the sale of stock, he sought ways
to improve Metro's image. By then he was a member of the Thrift
Advisory Committee to the Federal Reserve Board and was re-
elected for a second term in 1984. That position gave him an
opportunity to develop a relationship with Paul Volcker, chairman
of the board. Norm pointed out that high interest rates and low farm
commodity prices were the reasons why the farm economy did not
recover in 1983 and 1984 like other sectors did. The federal deficit

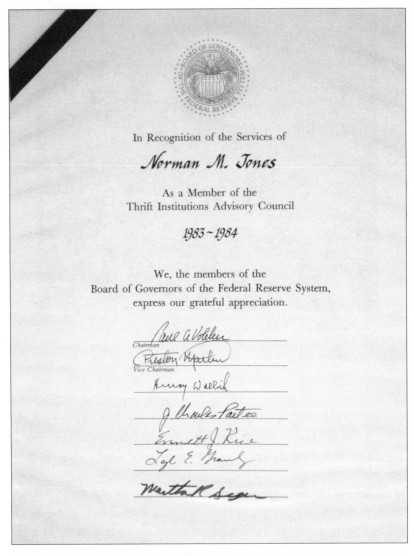

In Recognition of the Services of

Norman M. Jones

As a Member of the
Thrift Institutions Advisory Council

1983 ~ 1984

We, the members of the
Board of Governors of the Federal Reserve System,
express our grateful appreciation.

A certificate recognizing Norm's first term on the Thrift Institutions Advisory Council, 1983-1984. He was re-elected to this board and also served on four other national boards.

Supplemental Report
to the
Second Annual Report of the
Federal Savings and Loan Insurance Corporation
Industry Advisory Committee

to the

Committee on Banking, Finance and Urban Affairs
of the
United States House of Representatives

and the

Committee on Banking, Housing, and Urban Affairs
of the
United States Senate

Title page of the FSLICIAC report presented by Norm as chair to the Senate Banking Committee.

was the major cause of rising interest rates, because the government was in the market competing for funds. He also was on the executive committee of the U.S. League of Savings Institutions, which had given high priority to reducing the federal deficit.

Metro had total assets of $1.67 billion with a liquidity ratio of 9.4 percent and probably had a better computer system than most banks, all of which made Norm eager to move ahead. Norm was convinced that size and geographical diversification were imperative for success in the financial world. Metro was the largest financial institution in North Dakota, larger than the Bank of North Dakota, the North Dakota offices of Northwest Corporation, and First Bank System Inc., but it seemed stalemated. North Dakota no longer offered the possibilities for growth that Norm desired. He was looking at the three- or four-state area.

Members of the Federal Reserve Board, seated. Chairman Paul Volcher, center. Members of the Advisory Council, standing. Norm, second from left in back row.

In 1984 he had two good breaks. First, the FHLB granted Metro approval to become a federal stock savings bank and it was renamed Metropolitan Federal Bank fsb. (MFB) in July. Norm said, "We think that it was quite a plus . . . you could advertise yourself as a bank." His second good break came when federal regulators, who had frowned on acquisitions across state lines, changed their stance and out-state buyers were being encouraged to buy ailing S&Ls. Fortunately for Norm, Mitchell Home Savings of Mitchell, South Dakota, was in serious trouble, and it was purchased in late 1984. Morrie was very involved; often he was the lead person in making contact with ailing institutions that were looking for a buyer or to be merged. He understood the plight of those associations and was probably Norm's equal in making their officers comfortable about being part of Metropolitan.

To handle the extra work load, management was restructured. Effective December 31, 1984, Norm resigned as President and was promoted to Chairman and Chief Executive Officer of MFB, Bill Nilles became President and Chief Operating

Norm with President Ronald Reagan, featured speaker at the national S&L convention.

Officer, and Gary Dietz, Executive Vice President. Morrie, Corporate Secretary and Executive Vice President for Corporate Development, was elected to the board to fill the unexpired term of Ray Whiting, who had retired.

Norm closed his report for that quarter: "We look toward the future as a period of significant change and opportunity for Metropolitan Federal and the entire financial services industry." He no doubt had a feeling of satisfaction to note that the FHLB of Des Moines required that an association had to have liquid investments

121

Nancy Reagan and Eunice Jones at the White House.

of at least 5 percent of net withdrawable deposits, plus short-term borrowing, for Metro's ratio was 7.88 percent. Metro was prepared for change, which came rapidly. The August 18-21, 1984, *Financial World* had named Metropolitan one of America's top twenty-five growth companies for the past five years. It was one of only two financial companies on the list.

Bartkowski felt that Norm was one of the smartest and most intuitive persons he had ever met. He was quick to grasp an idea and was the kind of executive that did not need a great deal of preparation. "He was fun to work with and so quick to catch on." He continued with an illustration. In 1984 MSMC became the general partner on the Fargo Radisson Hotel project. Metropolitan

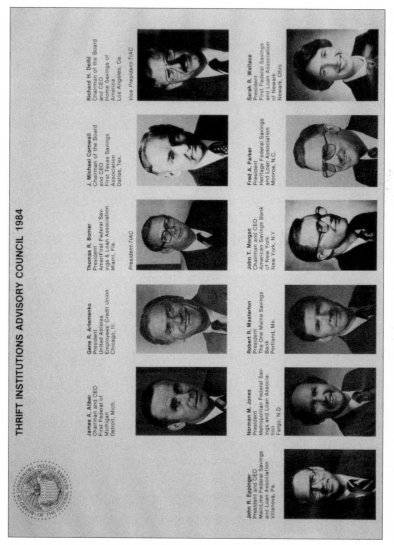

THRIFT INSTITUTIONS ADVISORY COUNCIL 1984

James A. Aliber
Chairman and CEO
First Federal of
Michigan
Detroit, Mich.

Gene R. Artemenko
President
United Airlines
Employees' Credit Union
Chicago, Ill.

Thomas R. Bomar
President
AmeriFirst Federal Sav-
ings & Loan Association
Miami, Fla.

President-TIAC

J. Michael Cornwall
Chairman of the Board
and CEO
First Texas Savings
Association
Dallas, Tex.

Richard H. Deihl
Chairman of the Board
and CEO
Home Savings of
America
Los Angeles, Ca.

Vice President-TIAC

John R. Eppinger
President and CEO
MainLine Federal Savings
and Loan Association
Villanova, Pa.

Norman M. Jones
President
Metropolitan Federal Sav-
ings and Loan Associa-
tion
Fargo, N.D.

Robert R. Masterton
President
The One Maine Savings
Bank
Portland, Me.

John T. Morgan
Chairman and CEO
American Savings Bank
of New York
New York, N.Y.

Fred A. Parker
President
Heritage Federal Savings
and Loan Association
Monroe, N.C.

Sarah R. Wallace
President
First Federal Savings
and Loan Association
of Newark
Newark, Ohio

Thrift Institutions Advisory Council, 1984, during Norm's first term.

123

Federal was to occupy the top four floors of the eighteen-story structure. In spring 1985, when the exterior work was completed, there was a scheduled TV news conference that was to feature Norm on the roof with the traditional Christmas tree. Everything was put on hold because Norm was not around. He was off helping a young couple open a savings account. "That is the kind of person he was." Gary Dietz, who worked closely with Norm on the management committee, said, "Norm's enthusiasm was unbelievable. He was a real do-er, which carried over to the people he worked with."

The Norm and Bill team did not change after Metro went public. Board members observed how Norm saw the opportunities in growth and passed the details to Bill to work out the problems and put the new acquisition into operation. Director Bill Marcil commented about the professional respect those two had for each other, plus they were good friends, which gave Metro a great period of leadership. Doug Larsen said that board members often grilled them about some of the acquisitions or mergers that were being planned. They quickly learned that Norm and Bill had done their homework and were able to defend their position. He added that Norm and Bill made a "very smooth" transition to being a public company. Norm saw the opportunities but was too soft to be the hatchet man, while Bill could solve the money problems and be tough with personnel if they were not doing their job, but neither of them ever showed any anger.

Dave Lysne, Director of Human Resources, commented that Metro's labor turnover rate while still in Fargo was less than half of the national rate because of the family atmosphere cultivated by Norm, Morrie, and the top officers. Lysne recalled that Norm and Eunice invited Lysne and his wife to accompany them to a national convention where they were treated "like their children. It was a great working environment." Lysne noted that it seemed as if everyone at the convention knew Norm, to which Doug Larsen replied that Norm was an excellent P.R. person, a great networker, and he just naturally made connections. Bob Clark, head of the computer department, added that one of the real hidden assets of the Metro culture was that it had little "run-off" from its acquired companies. He explained. Usually when an institution was merged or acquired, it was normal to lose a high percent of its customer base, but Metro's leadership and culture made the acquired customers feel comfortable and they stayed aboard. "This was a real key to our rapid growth."[3]

On Wall Street

Nineteen eighty-four was another good year for Metro compared to what many of the thrifts were still experiencing. Metro earned a gross income of $156 million, originated $226 million in mortgage loans and $62 million in other loans, and purchased another $163 million in loans. Assets increased to $1.45 billion, and its liquidity ratio was a healthy 8.16 percent. The first service expansion in 1985 was joining FASTBANK, a five-state Automatic Teller Machine (ATM) network.

After securing the Mitchell S&L, Metro was established in South Dakota and put the company in a position to acquire what Norm had watched for many months. In February 1985 he purchased Dakota Savings and Loan in Sioux Falls and its branches in Flandreau and Salem, giving him a good foothold in that part of the state. At the same time, the top management was being restructured to handle the anticipated increase in activity, and by March 1, 1985, the organization of a holding company, Metropolitan Financial Corporation (MFC), was completed.

Penny Dobbin, portfolio manager for *Barron's*, wrote in the March 25, 1985, issue that Metropolitan was one of the "five most intriguing investment opportunities in the industry. . . . It is one company that could prove me wrong in my statement that thrifts will not do a good job making commercial non-real estate loans." The *Barron's* report was followed in August when Robert Chaut of Salomon Brothers announced: "We expect the shares of Metropolitan to out-perform the market in the next six to twelve months." On November 18, 1985, after being on the NASDAQ since March 1983, MFC had its IPO and became a member of the New York Stock Exchange (NYSE). It was the first North Dakota company to be listed along with over 1,500 companies on "the big board."

During a television interview after the announcement, Norm stated, "If the stock does well, look for Metropolitan to expand into Iowa and Nebraska and perhaps beyond. We want to be a Midwest company. In order to handle all that, it would take some additional

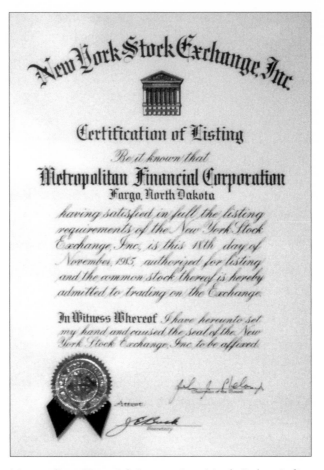

New York Stock Exchange, Inc.

Certification of Listing

Be it known that

Metropolitan Financial Corporation
Fargo, North Dakota

having satisfied in full the listing requirements of the New York Stock Exchange, Inc., is this 18th day of November, 1985, authorized for listing and the common stock thereof is hereby admitted to trading on the Exchange.

In Witness Whereof *I have hereunto set my hand and caused the seal of the New York Stock Exchange, Inc. to be affixed.*

Metropolitan Financial Corporation, North Dakota's first company to be listed on the NYSE.

capital in years to come and there may need to be some additional stock [sold]."

The year was capped off on December 2, 1985, when the company had the good fortune of having the third state in Norm's plans opened to him. Regulators were looking for a buyer for the ailing Midland Federal Savings and Loan Association of Moorhead, Minnesota. Metro did not need an office only a mile from its home office because it already had many customers on the east side of the Red River, but now it gained the rights to establish or acquire other branches in the state. Probably, more importantly, it was a door-opener to the Twin Cities.[4]

Assets Hit $2 Billion

The company received a great deal of publicity throughout 1985 because of acquiring the Mitchell S&L in South Dakota, becoming a public company listed on the NYSE, and by acquiring its first Minnesota thrift, which presented opportunities for further acquisitions. The farm economy was not particularly bright as 1986 opened, which meant that chances weren't high for improved deposits in the Dakotas. In February Metro applied to the FHLBB for permission to open a branch in the Twin Cities area, and on April 16 it received approval to do so. As a result of that action, a branch office in Edina was opened, which exposed Metro to the larger Twin Cities area.

Soon an agreement was reached with Kmart stores through franchises with First Nationwide Network of Atlanta to open some unique branches. Franchises were purchased from First Nationwide for Minnesota and the two Dakotas. A survey of the Kmart clientele indicated that they were an excellent customer base, and an agreement was reached with First Nationwide to establish a number of low overhead offices in the Twin Cities.

In May 1986 five kiosks (booths) were opened. The kiosks, which took up an area of only 136 square feet each, were economical to operate, and they exposed Metro to customers that it might not otherwise have come into contact with. The reasoning behind the kiosks was that fifteen could be built for one-fourth the cost of one traditional brick-and-mortar office. Kiosks in some of the best locations in California Kmarts generated $4 to $5 million in deposits annually, and soon booths in the Twin Cities were performing at that level. In the first nine months, five kiosks generated $26 million in new deposits. Another five were opened in September and by the end of December, they had generated $3 million in new deposits.

The booths were a bare-bones bank staffed by sales people who worked on commission. "It was their job to sell accounts." Applications were filled out on the spot and sent to the office in Edina. Initially, the kiosks had no cash available except through ATMs provided by the FASTBANK network. Later, they were enlarged to handle savings and checking accounts. Because the kiosks were so easy to establish and efficient to operate, Metro could offer a quarter to a half percent higher interest rates on deposits than their competitors in the Twin Cities market. Metro soon considered opening more Kmart booths in skyways and even in the Rothschild headquarters located in St. Paul, plus in Duluth, Rochester, St. Cloud, larger communities in the Dakotas, along with two or three additional full-service offices in the Twin Cities.

When Norm was asked why Metro was so interested in expanding into the Twin Cities, he replied that western North Dakota was experiencing a combined agricultural and energy depression that could hurt many loans, especially in real estate and motels impacted by the weakened economy. The two Dakotas combined only had 1.2 million people and its thirty-one offices were getting most of the available deposits. The company needed new deposits to provide mortgage money for its loan offices in Arizona, California, Colorado, and Florida, so it turned to the Twin Cities area, which had 2 million people and would be a good source for new funds.

Norm realized that for safety reasons Metro had to have more geographic and economic diversity plus a larger base to make it easier to grow. The company added to its reserves while other financial institutions were depleting theirs. From 1985 to 1986 it increased its reserves from 4.26 to 5.35 percent—a growth of 25 percent—and by December 1986 it had $108 million in legal reserves and an additional $16 million in special loss reserves.

While the above action was taking place, a Financial Services Department was organized to offer tax-deferred annuities. A three-for-two stock split was declared, which gave Metro 3.6 million shares outstanding. That was followed by a second stock floatation, which raised $16.5 million, making a total of nearly $40 million raised by the 1983 and 1986 offerings.

Not everything attempted in 1986 went the way management planned. Metropolitan tried to buy or merge with First Minnesota Savings Bank in the Twin Cities with $3.1 billion in assets, the third largest in Minnesota. After months of negotiation, both sides soon realized that it was not a good fit. Ben Crabtree, securities analyst for Dain Bosworth, suggested that "First Minnesota was too large for Metro to swallow. It was just too big and too complex. It would have been very hard to finance, and, I suspect, very hard to integrate." It was very appealing, but as one of the Metro directors implied, the First Minnesota people had the attitude that "they were not going to let a small town group of business people buy them out."

By this time Metro leaders realized that having a company management team in the Twin Cities "would be important to future expansion. . . . [But the *Forum* reporter was assured that moving to Minneapolis] is not in the plans for our organization." By November 1986 things had progressed so well and so rapidly that Norm was preparing for a move to the Twin Cities, and Morrie asked Bartkowski to establish a position in Minneapolis.

During 1986 there was discussion that Metro should consider expanding into Wisconsin because that would probably be an easier market to penetrate than the Twin Cities. However, after reviewing Wisconsin's regulations, it was decided that it would be easier to compete in the Twin Cities. Metro was determined to broaden its presence in the Twin Cities and took a major step when it purchased the 102-year-old Rothschild Financial Corporation. Rothschild was a mortgage bank that had about three times Metro's mortgage business. The purchase put Metro among the 100 largest mortgage banking firms in the nation. This gave Metro a strong mortgage banking operation, which greatly helped it penetrate the Twin Cities market. A *St. Paul Pioneer Press* writer speculated that Metro paid $25 million for Rothschild, which had a mortgage service portfolio of $1.5 billion and in 1986 had generated $500 million in new business. It was expected to have "even more business in 1987." In addition to the Twin Cities, Rothschild also had eight offices in Colorado, Florida, Iowa, Kansas, and Nebraska.

Long-time board member Dick Kvamme was called on to display his expertise in construction when projects "went bad." One of the most serious came in 1986. Prior to being purchased by Metro, Rothschild had made a loan to a developer in Ann Arbor, Michigan, who failed. When Kvamme got to the construction site, he found "a hole in the ground with twenty feet of footings poured." He assessed the situation, determined what had to be done, and engaged a new contractor. Metro's loan was $5 million. Kvamme concluded that Metro came out of that loan "Okay, but not as good as on some of the S&Ls that they acquired later." According to Mike Nilles, Rothschild had made many bad loans to that developer and then passed them on to Metro. "They were of a different culture."

Everyone who worked with Norm commented that they never saw him get angry, but Bill Marcil admitted that he once saw him upset over a personnel problem. "He was disappointed with the behavior of a ranking employee." Norm was extremely patient with Rothschild, but Doug Larsen recalled that finally in 1989 "Norm called the pilot and said we are going to St. Paul and settle that. He took the bull by the horns and actually axed a couple of their leaders." Jordahl related to that event: "Rothschild took Metro off its mission for a brief period, but after Norm made some changes, they adopted Metro's philosophy." Then, the mortgage company was renamed Metropolitan Financial Mortgage Corporation.

Later, Kvamme went to Vail, Colorado, where two investors were involved in building a shopping center and asked if they could borrow a "couple hundred thousand more." Kvamme was sent to investigate and to determine the problem. He met with the accountant, who was working for someone else in the center but not for the investors, and learned that the general contractor was not responding to make corrections. Kvamme called on the defaulting contractor and the remaining work was finished. This had a happy ending; the accountant's employers bought the builder's interest and Metro cleared $80,000 on the transaction.

In 1986 Metro experienced a 115 percent increase over 1985 with earnings of $22 million and topped $2 billion in assets with a liquidity ratio of 10 percent, making it one of the fifty largest thrift/holding companies in the nation. Norm told the *Forum* reporter that good planning in previous years had provided for the success in 1986. Others credited him for "his keenness in advanced planning while some financial experts called him a visionary." The 1986 issue of *Financial World* polled chief executives of companies with more that $100 million in sales, and Norm was ranked "the third best S&L executive in the country."[5]

The Loss of Morrie

When Norm started with Metro in 1952, he was the seventh employee and recalled that he did every job from cleaning the office to being teller. "You got a chance to know a little bit about everything in the business. I would take an application, make an appraisal, and close the loan. And in between, maybe talk the customer into opening a savings account." When he started his thirty-fifth year in 1987, the company had thirty-one offices in North Dakota, three in South Dakota, two in Iowa—Waterloo and

Cedar Rapids, both of which were later merged into other offices. After acquiring Moorhead, Minnesota, Norm was free to expand to the Twin Cities, where they added kiosks and a mortgage office.

New deposits grew by more than $67 million during 1987, much of which came because of expansion and the balance from continued emphasis on quality of customer service. In addition, two balance sheet transactions took place to better position the company "to withstand the volatile and uncertain interest rate environment of the time." The first transaction came when the company sold mortgage-backed securities and repaid high rate long-term borrowing. The profits gained were used to offset pre-payment penalties. The second move came when Metro was able to repay long-term funds it had borrowed from the FHLB at considerably lower cost than those that were repaid, and the funds were used to purchase additional mortgage-backed securities. This resulted in much enhanced net income. By December 1987 assets had grown to $2.3 billion, which placed Metro among the top seventy-five thrift holding companies in the nation.

Despite all the euphoria caused by the considerable progress during the year, 1987 ended in a cloud of despair that probably changed the course of the company. In 1984 Morrie had been diagnosed with cancer, but he "continued working in his usual enthusiastic manner." Bill Bartkowski commented that Morrie went to work every day because he felt that he was going to lick it. He had great ability and was a very diligent worker who rose through the ranks rapidly. Everyone who knew him realized that he felt strongly about being a leader and a role model. One day Morrie told Bartkowski that his cancer was worse and he was going to start a more aggressive treatment. Up to that time Bartkowski had worked almost exclusively with Morrie, but from then on he worked with Norm.

Norm was later asked if he and Morrie had ever discussed succession, to which he commented, "We and the board had never formally discussed the issue, but we all more or less felt that he was the logical successor." Nancy stated that Norm was really hit when Morrie died. It was like the rug had been pulled out from under him "because he was so confident about how well Morrie was doing."

The following letters from two friends describe Morrie as objectively as is possible. Trueman Tryhus, who had known the

Jones family since the 1950s from several perspectives, wrote to Morrie on November 11, 1987. He addressed it to "Young Timer" and started with regrets that he had never acknowledged previously.

> I have never relayed the deep respect and admiration I hold for you. Specifically your selfless courage and unyielding Christian faith. You have taught me much in these past many months as you so stoically and patiently continue to battle this illness that challenges you. Unbelievably, you never display any self pity, and particularly you never have any questions of God's grace. . . . God obviously recognizes great strength in you as he uses you to teach the rest of us how a brave and true Christian responds to adversity. . . . You very definitely are one of God's blessings, and particularly for me you are a resource of strength for sustaining and building upon my faith. I especially thank you for that.

The following is from a eulogy by Howard Dahl, one of Morrie's very closest friends during his last decade, given at Morrie's funeral on December 15, 1987.

> We who were close to Morrie Jones well know that few people could ever approach his level of kindness. For years he and I were part of a group that met weekly for prayer and Bible study. The rest of us recognized Morrie as a man with a strong, vibrant, and growing faith. . . . Morrie had a vital, growing desire to give proclamation to his faith. He was concerned for friends and acquaintances who did not recognize life's spiritual dimension. Over the past few years, many lives have been touched for eternity by Morrie's witness.

Nancy reminisced about Morrie's last months.

> He had his priorities right—God, family, work. He was a great father—firm but fun! He was an avid reader and set a great example for his children. It was important to him to have a lake place—I think he knew death was ahead and wanted to have that time together. He had a unique approach to death. I never once heard him ask, "Why me?"

He looked at it as an opportunity to witness to other people as to how God works in our life. He was determined to carry out life without others noticing it. He put up a brave front—working full-time even between surgeries until his last three months in the hospital.

One can only speculate what Metro's future would have been if Morrie had lived. The following comments by three insiders only add more to the speculation. Tryhus, who knew Maurice Sr., Norm, and Morrie, said, "They were good, better, and best whichever way you line them up. If he had not died, Morrie could have taken over. But going from less than a million to $8 billion would have been hard to duplicate."

Noel Fedje, when asked about the future, replied by qualifying his answer with a historical perspective:

Norm was never overpaid. When you look at the results, the assets of Metro, when they sold, and the earnings record there is no way he could have been overpaid. I think there were times that the board could not grasp what he was doing.

After the retirement of Bill Nilles and the loss of Morrie, Norm turned to Eunice for his "sounding board." In addition to her three years at Metropolitan, she had worked at three other financial institutions and had a good understanding of the business. Close friends of Norm and Eunice all indicated that even though Eunice was "Mrs. Metropolitan," she did not need the recognition nor did she mind being in the background.

In retrospect Eunice said giving Norm comfort about the move to the Twin Cities was probably her most important contribution. She fully realized how lonely it was at the top.

Norm had many challenges but probably nothing caused him more agony than having to make a decision about having to move people to a different position or to a different community—i.e. the Twin Cities. Maybe those people did not realize that we prayed about them." She continued, "But on the other hand it was exciting and humbling to observe the accomplishments that he and the Metro employees achieved. They were a team of diligent people. We loved them all. Norman felt that every employee was significant. He made an effort to visit with everyone and show encouragement. He also had a great memory of and loyalty toward Metro customers and wanted to do the best for them.

When Eunice was asked about Norm's positive traits, she replied,

> Norman had a God-given inspiration. He was such an innovator. As he rose to the opportunities before him, he became so polished in his one-on-one conversation and then in public speaking that most people never realized that he had either a speaking or a reading problem.

Through his efforts he joined the ranks of many past and present leaders who have done the same on their journey to leadership. Eunice reflected on a conversation she had with an uncle. She repeated his words: "You know you are what Norman has become. You were born with common sense." The uncle observed that Norm was very optimistic and Eunice was more realistic, but she said that she never held him back.[6]

Moving To The Twin Cities

Except for the great loss of Morrie in December, 1987 was a year of laying a solid foundation in which Metro bucked the trend in the industry. The company was the target of some "anti" feeling from the local area bankers. Was it jealousy or the stigma that the S&Ls had from their recent past, or did the banks not like it that under new regulations the thrifts could be more competitive than they had been in the past? Some of the brokers in Fargo advised their clients not to purchase Metro stock. This writer can attest to that, for he received such advice from his banker and others in the finance industry.

Norm, like most entrepreneurs, ignored the criticism and continued on his journey, which included fulfilling his community obligations. In April 1988 he received the Fargo-Cass County Economic Development Corporation's "Economic Development" Award in recognition for his efforts in business development. This award was designed "to honor people who have made exemplary contributions to economic development." The citation read in part that in 1987 he had been chosen by the *Financial World* as one of the top three executives in the savings industry. In his typical manner, Norm "credited the officers and employees of the company with providing the environment that makes sound economic development possible. . . . The company you work for had to have a commitment for industrial development."

Much has been written about Norm and his style of management. In a previous chapter there was reference to his stuttering childhood years, but now he was recognized as a leader in the industry on the national scene. Eunice, who has probably heard him make more speeches than anyone, commented that he was often called to say a few words. "It is always as if he is inspired." Bartkowski and Beverly Austin, a senior vice president of MFB, both wrote speeches and other presentations for him and realized how quickly Norm grasped ideas. "He liked to speak to the key points and all we had to do was put them on the screen. He had all the data in his head to make a solid presentation." He proved to be a very effective speaker. Bartkowski said that both he and Austin often commented how much fun it was to work with him. "Sometimes he did not realize how hard some things were to do. He would make a deal and then we had to figure out to implement it. But you'd never say it couldn't be done."

Bartkowski recalled Norm saying, "Problems are a lot like monkeys." He did not like to have someone come in with a problem. "Don't be giving me your monkeys." He told lawyers how he wanted to do something and left them to figure out how to do it. As a parting thought on that subject, Bartkowski said that Beverly Austin was a real solution person, which accounted for the three of them having such a good working relationship.

Director Trueman Tryhus said that Norm could walk into any office and get the people to warm up to him in minutes. He could win over nearly everyone by showing them that he was there to help. "That is how he acquired so many firms so easily." Tryhus, who was in favor of moving to the Twin Cities, said Norm's tactics did not change there but it was obvious that there was a higher level of sophistication. Norm's approach was the key to why Metro was so successful throughout the Midwest and why the company had such a good customer retention after they acquired other institutions.

In early 1988 Bill Bartkowski and some of his colleagues moved to the Twin Cities. The culture was not the same, which was complicated by the fact that Metro was growing rapidly, and to avoid employing so many outsiders, workers from within were elevated to positions that were above their ability. This often hurt those individuals, but it was part of the price of growing. Many from Fargo were reluctant to transfer to the Cities, but because they had such good positions, they felt that they had no other choice because they wanted to stay with the company.

Bill Marcil, president of Forum Publishing Company and a board member, was impressed by the strong ethical focus that the entire family possessed. They were risk takers but there was never a question about the bounds within which they operated. Marcil had experience on other boards, both on a local basis and nationally. He was on a bank board and quickly realized that it was "purely a rubber stamp, so [he] resigned from it. What was the purpose of being on it?" He was also on the National Chamber of Commerce board, which was very large and run by a paid executive. "It was no fun but they needed to put on a show of national representation." He stated that the Metro board was different because the members had real input.

> Norm was in charge but he was like an outside person. He was such a visionary. We all felt comfortable about speaking up and Norm accepted a great deal of input from us. I remember being on the compensation committee and did not see Norm's name on it and mentioned it to him. He said, "I am doing okay. It is not a problem." I disagreed with that thinking because he was doing a great job and should be paid for it.

Director Marcil commented that "some of the family culture was lost in the move but it was the right move for the company. If you are going to grow, the leadership had to rub shoulders with other leaders in the industry. This move proved to be a real benefit for the shareholders and Norm was very concerned about their welfare." Mike Nilles, who sat in on the board meetings, marveled how the board and management operated on a consensus basis about moving to the Twin Cities. "There might have been a dissenting vote on an issue but I cannot recall any. The board never got into micro-management. The questions came from the administration and the board added their combined wisdom." Noel Fedje realized that Norm well understood the benefit to stockholders by moving to Minneapolis where stock traded for at least seven times earnings, in New York it was ten times earnings, while in Fargo stock traded only at five times earnings.[7]

Six Institutions In One Purchase

At the long-range strategy sessions, it was determined that the crisis in the industry offered opportunities for Metro to expand. Its conservative method of operation had kept it from avoiding some of the risky pitfalls that hurt many S&Ls and enabled it to maintain strong reserves. Strict criteria had been established for assessing and evaluating insolvent institutions before attempting to make any acquisitions. Any new acquisition had to be in a contiguous market where Metro already had operating experience. If the prospective acquisition had a negative net worth, the FSLIC would have to provide sufficient assistance to remove the deficient position to protect Metro's future earnings and capital from risk. In return for assistance from the FHLBB and FSLIC, Metro would have to bring, the acquired institutions up to minimum capital requirements. It would also manage "a significant number of problem assets for the FSLIC and share the profits and losses on realized assets with the FSLIC." Metro would also be responsible for effective management, sound lending practices, responsible deposit solicitation and gathering practices, as well as exemplary customer service. The FSLIC knew that Metro was capable of all of the above and was comfortable working with it.

In mid-1988 the FSLIC offered six thrifts for sale in Metro's area. Norm stated that these six were first offered individually but none of them sold, so he suggested to the Des Moines regional office to put all six in one package and they could be sold individually or as a package. He knew that some commercial banks were interested in purchasing units, but he understood that it was more efficient for the FSLIC to sell them as a unit. Metro was the only bidder with the resources to handle the package and it put in the highest bid. Bartkowski described the six as "terribly troubled, but there were notes from the government to sweeten the deal."

Norm did not want to deplete company resources, so FSLIC offered notes for $366.6 million to make up for the negative net worth of the acquired institutions. Another note for $190.7 million covered loans that consisted of real estate owned and in judgment, delinquent loans, and investments in and advances to subsidiary companies. Plus, it also took over the foreclosed loans. The notes were due within ten years, but the FSLIC had the option to redeem them any time for cash. During the duration of the notes, they earned interest of 1 percent over the six-month Treasury bill rate. In addition, a yield maintenance fee was paid on the covered assets at a rate from 1.75 to 2.75 percent over the average Treasury bill rate. This meant that if the Treasury bills yielded 4 percent, Metro could earn up to an additional 2.75 percent for a total of 6.75 percent on the FSLIC notes. The FSLIC also agreed to share in the gains or losses on certain covered assets. All Metro income from the FSLIC was non-taxable under the Internal Revenue Code, which in 1988 was $15.2 million.

The acquisition, which took place August 26, 1988, was standard procedure to reduce the work load for the government in getting troubled institutions back into operation immediately. It lessened the monetary risk for the government by minimizing potential losses for the public. Bartkowski commented that it was Norm's way of doing business that helped solve the problems for the others. He cut deals that helped Metro, the government, and the people he bought out. He seemed to understand the ebb and flow of interest rates and kept Metro strong while doing so.

The Forum of September 3, 1988, announced, "Metropolitan Federal Growth Bucks Industry Trend" and stated it was one of the strongest financial institutions in the upper Midwest. The company had flourished even though it was located in an agricultural area that had experienced drought and a prolonged recession at a time when the savings and loan industry nationwide was plagued with insolvent institutions.

M. Danny Wall, chairman of the FHLBB, the governing board of the nation's savings and loan associations, knew that Metro was a well-managed organization that had built its business in a very straightforward manner and in a "rather conservative fashion." The above transaction included S&Ls in Brainerd, Grand Rapids, Hibbing, Owatonna, and Stillwater in Minnesota, and Mason City, Iowa, and made MFC eligible to receive as much as $299 million to aid in the conversion. The acquisition gave the company ninety-four branch offices in four states with assets of $3.7 billion, and an increase of 120 percent in deposits from over 200,000 new accounts. Equally important, acquiring the Iowa firm gave Metro the legal right to expand into Iowa, Wisconsin, and Arizona.

Wall commented that the purchase was an asset for the FHLB in its efforts to resolve the problems of the troubled thrifts nationwide. He had appointed Norm as chairman of the national advisory committee of the FSLIC in 1978 because he knew from his Fargo days how well Norm had managed Metro and the knowledge he had of the industry. Wall reported that progress was being made to find solutions for the troubled thrifts through merger, sale, or insurance payoff to the depositors, of which the first two were preferred. As of August 1988 the corner had not yet been turned, but progress was being made. He knew that Norm brought a wide range of expertise and had "a good Middle America approach to doing business."

The Minneapolis corporate office was opened in the Lincoln Centre at 333 South Seventh Street in downtown Minneapolis staffed by Beverly Austin and Bill Bartkowski with Norm dividing his time between there and Fargo. At that time 42 percent of Metro's savings were from North Dakota, 41 percent from Minnesota, 13 percent from Iowa, and 3 percent from South Dakota, but with the new acquisitions, the company's marketing territory changed considerably. Minneapolis was where the action was, but it also gave Metro more exposure to the media.

An article by Steve Brook in *St. Paul Pioneer Press* entitled "N.D. Thrift Makes Acquisitions Work: Firm Acquires 6 Insolvent Thrifts, But Very Little Risk" gave additional insights of what others less friendly than *The Forum* thought of the deal. Brook continued that Metropolitan had avoided huge losses and charges of mismanagement that plagued the industry, but:

> Analysts think it recently pulled off a deal so good it amounts to a legal form of bank robbery. . . . Analysts were amazed at the generosity of the deal. . . . It's a tremendous deal. . . . Another said, "It's a really neat deal". . . . The somewhat embarrassing kicker is what Metropolitan paid. . . . Shrewd, deadpanned one analyst. . . . The bottom line . . . "We're going to make a lot of money" . . . said a Metropolitan official.

The article speculated about how much longer the FSLIC would continue to "give away these sweet deals? The FSLIC made up the negative equity. . . ." Stock analysts concluded that Metro's earnings should skyrocket and encouraged "buy" recommendations. In addition to other gains, the company would have improved economies of scale because it would be able to consolidate "back-office operations and lay off top-level managers of the acquired companies."

Norm commented,

> People are bound to come up with the question, "If all of a sudden we can improve our earnings by that much, what did the government give away?" But we don't think we got any better deal than anybody bidding for failed thrifts in California or Texas. . . . Other bidders had the same opportunity but wanted more federal assistance. Maybe they were scared of what they were bidding on. They were commercial bankers. They were individual investment people. They didn't understand our business, how to turn it around or cut expenses.

Norm defended what the FSLIC did because they would not have been able to manage the troubled institutions as well as a well-run S&L could.

The analysts agreed that Metropolitan was the right company in the right place at the right time with the right bid for an eager seller. Another analyst stated that the problems had to be taken care of quickly with someone who had had success in acquisitions. Metro had been doing that since 1982, and it was doing it in its familiar rural setting. Brook added that Metro was one of the first to benefit from the FSLIC program of negative equity, which Norm understood; he was comfortable taking the FSLIC IOUs because he had full faith in the federal government. He said that Metro's external auditors made a comment in their audit about the validity of those notes. Norm also realized from his time spent in Washington that the FSLIC was under pressure from politicians to get the thrift problem solved, and it did not have the resources to handle all the defaulting S&Ls.

Norm said, "I think they're [FSLIC] doing as good a job as they can. In order to get capital into the industry, they have to make it so you can make money. . . . Otherwise who will come in and take over?" The FSLIC offices in Des Moines and Washington both concurred that Metro's offer was cheaper for them than liquidating the institutions and paying off the depositors. They could open for business immediately but their biggest problem—non-performing loans—would take at least five years to clear up. Norm assured everyone that Metro had an adequate staff to manage the acquisitions and that it was not through expanding. Bartkowski, who was in charge of the Twin City office, realized what all the new branches it had gained as spin-offs from the Stillwater and Owatonna S&Ls plus the Kmart kiosks meant to Metro's presence in the greater metropolitan region.

Linette Hartman, who worked in the mortgage department, recalled that the greatest change that she observed after going public was that "we became more conscious about what the quarterly earnings per share were going to be." She commented that the culture in the Fargo office was "great; everyone was so upbeat and with all the growth the place seemed so full of opportunity." But as soon as Rothschild was purchased and in 1988 when some employees were shifted to the Twin Cities, one department at a time, morale drooped. Many did not want to leave Fargo. Hartman moved to the main accounting department of Metro Bank while some received transfers to other out-state locations. Those who did not want to move to the Twin Cities and could not be relocated within the company were provided with help to find other positions and a good severance package.

There was always pressure that had not been so obvious earlier but Rod Jordahl, the mortgage department head, handled it well. Each month he had to take the earnings report up to Norm. If the department had been working especially hard to get a report out, he frequently came up with a department party to relieve the tension. Buying the troubled thrifts always called for extra work. "It seems like so many had been part of some big loans that had gone bad." Hartman said that her colleagues were all salaried employees so there was no monetary incentive—except for year-end bonuses—for working many extra hours "but we all felt so good about being part of a team with a company that was really going places." Employee attitude was so good that whenever acquisitions were made, there was "night work as late as 2 a.m., but they were excited about what was taking place." Jordahl added that everyone realized what was happening and they had lots of pride about it. The most memorable department party was when Jordahl had the group over to his house after the six institutions were purchased in one deal and had T-shirts printed that read: "We Survived the Year of Acquisitions."

Norm's final goal for the year came November 30 when MFC paid $25 million to acquire Edina Realty, Edina Financial Services, and Equity Title Services, Inc. Edina Financial was the number one mortgage originator in the Twin Cities and Equity Title was the largest residential title company in Minnesota and the fourth largest company of its kind in the nation. It had thirty offices, 1,500 sales associates, and 700 employees. This provided Metro with thirty-two established offices to accommodate new savings customers at a very low investment. This gave Metro an opening to broaden its financial services and provided an "enlarged source for mortgage loan and home financing." Norm said that Edina Realty was a rare vertical integration for a thrift company that involved about 40 percent of the homes sold in the Multiple Listing Service. Through that connection MFC did business with about 40 percent of Edina Realty's home buyers.

Norm's goal for 1988 was exceeded when on December 28 the failed First Financial Savings Bank of Des Moines, with assets of $262.7 million, was purchased. This acquisition included First Realty, Iowa's largest realty company. First Realty was immediately sold to Edina Realty, which temporarily gave it a strong presence in Iowa.

At year's end Metro had 1,100 employees in 104 branches, a 120 percent increase in deposits to $2.5 million, and $4.073 billion in assets. The company had changed from being the largest savings bank in North Dakota to a rapidly growing Midwestern financial organization of retail banking, mortgage investment, and real estate brokerage. It was a profitable year, which was shared by its stockholders who received a 10 percent stock dividend in July. Another 10 percent stock dividend was declared for the first quarter of 1989. In addition, the value of its common stock had increased by 75 percent.[8]

~ ~ ~ ~ ~

1. James R. Barth, *The Great Savings and Loan Debacle*, (Washington, D.C. The American Enterprise Institute,1991) pp. 1-4, hereafter Barth; Dietz interview; Mike Nilles interview.

2. Norman Jones interview; Offering Circular, Metropolitan Federal Savings and Loan Association of Fargo, March 24, 1983, pp. 6, 8, 9, 18, 36-37, 51, hereafter Prospectus; *Metropolitan Federal 1983 Annual Report*, pp.1, 3, 8, 11, hereafter Annual Report; Fedje interview; Dietz interview; *Metro Line*, June, 1984; interview of William P. Bartkowski, Minnetonka, Minnesota, May 31, 2007, hereafter Bartkowski interview; *Minneapolis Star*, June 14, 1987; Jordahl interview; interview of William C. Marcil, Fargo, May 15, 2007, hereafter Marcil interview; Larsen interview; *Fortune Magazine*, September, 19, 1983, p. 172.

3. Bartkowski interview; *Metro Line*, April, December, 1984 ; Dietz interview; Larsen interview; Lysne interview; Bill Nilles interview; Fedje interview; *The Forum*, January 1985; Annual Report, 1984, 1985; Clark interview; *The Minneapolis Star*, June 14, 1987; Metro History, p. 18.

4. Metro History, p. 19-20; Annual Report, 1984,1985; Corporate Highlights July 1986; Jordahl interview; Jones Scrapbook entitled, "Going Public."

5. Corporate Highlights July 1986; *The Forum*, January 31, 1987; *Minneapolis Star & Tribune*, June 14, 1987; Larsen interview; Mike Nilles, interview; *St. Paul Pioneer Press*, June 8, 1987; *Metro Line*, June 1987, January 1988; Ihry interview; interview of Linette Hartman, Fargo, March 13, 2007, hereafter Hartman interview; Kvamme interview; Metro History. p. 2; Annual Report, 1986.

6. *Minneapolis Star & Tribune*, June 14, 1987; *Metro Line*, August 1987; *St. Paul Pioneer Press*, June 8, 1987; Hartman interview; Metro History, p. 22; Skurdall-Jones, p.102; Trueman Tryhus, letter to Morrie Jones, November 11, 1987; Howard Dahl, Eulogy for Morrie Jones, December 15, 1987; Schafer interview; Tryhus interview; Mike Nilles interview; Fedje interview; Eunice Jones interview.

7. *The Forum*, April 14, 1988; Bartkowski interview; Tryhus interview; Lysne interview; Marcil interview; Fedje interview; Mike Nilles interview; Larsen interview.

8. Norman Jones interview; Bartkowski interview; Hartman interview; *The Forum*, September 3, 1988; Metro History, pp. 23-24; *St. Paul Pioneer Press*, December 26, 1988, Jordahl interview; Skurdall-Jones, p. 104; *Metro Line*, December 1988; Annual Report, 1988.

Chapter VI

Fourteen States and 220 Branches 1989-1995

The Financial Institutions Reform, Recovery, and Enforcement Act and Metropolitan's Reaction

The December 31, 1988, report of the FSLIC advisory committee, which Norm chaired, indicated that from 1980 through 1988 they had worked with 399 institutions that had been merged and with ninety-two others that were liquidated. Federal aid was needed to solve the problem, and on August 9, 1989, FIRREA, as it was known by the industry, became law. Norm, from his connection in Washington, knew what it would mean to the industry and prepared Metro for what was ahead.

Metro's goals for 1990 were: increase net worth; expand Metro's geographic area and market share; emphasize more predictable income, especially interest income; manage credit risk by limiting lending to areas related to housing and consumer finance; control interest rate risk; and integrate mortgage banking with real estate brokerage companies to become more effective providers of home mortgage credit. In his annual report to Metro stockholders, Norm explained what the company had done in the past year and how that had improved its position.

FIRREA imposed new regulatory capital requirements on thrift institutions effective December 7, 1989, with more stringent requirements effective July 1, 1994: (1) tangible requirements had to meet 1.5 percent of tangible assets by December 31, 1989, and exceed 3 percent by 1994; (2) core tangible capital, which included goodwill related to acquisitions prior to April 1989, to meet or exceed 3 percent of assets; and (3) risk-based reserves had to meet or exceed 6.4 percent of risk-adjusted capital by December 31, 1989, and 8 percent

Fargo Forum cartoon.

by 1994. Norm stated in the 1989 report that Metro had already attained the 12.6 percent level of risk-based capital, a clear indication of how sound it was. The statement indicated that in 1989, interest income from FSLIC notes had increased to $53.1 million, up $38 million from 1988. He added that in all respects the company had already fully phased in capital requirements of FIRREA.

FHLB's primary regulation was transferred to the Treasury Department and the FSLIC insurance fund to the FDIC. In 1990 the Resolution Trust Corporation (RTC) was created and provided with $50 billion, of which $40 billion was provided to aid the still-insolvent S&Ls and $10 billion to replenish the insurance fund.

The Affordable Housing Program provided funds to the FHLB to finance home ownership by individual families with incomes below 80 percent of the norm for the area to purchase, construct, or rehabilitate rental housing. At least 20 percent of the households had to have incomes below 50 percent of the median income for the area. The FIRREA regulation required that risk-based capital as a percent of risk-adjusted assets had to be at least 8 percent. That percent had to be maintained in hope of strengthening the institutions which would reduce the liability of the deposit insurance fund. Industry experts stated that the higher levels would be difficult to achieve because capital could only be raised through earnings and by selling stock. They maintained that was virtually impossible in the existing economic environment, so the law would only worsen the industry's problem.

The report indicated that the number of S&Ls was down to 3,011, and $10.825 billion in bonds had been issued to recapitalize the FSLIC in a newly established financing corporation referred to as FICO. As of May 9, 1989, nine of the twelve Federal Reserve districts indicated that they had a potential shortfall of $490,970,000, of which the Des Moines district had a total of $57,182,000. It was projected that from 1989 through 1998, about $51 billion would be needed for future interest payments of the FSLIC notes, indicating that the problem was far from solved.

In 1988 Metro had gained fifty-six banking offices, giving it a total of 105 offices in the two Dakotas, Iowa, Minnesota, and Wisconsin. In 1989 it opened a branch banking office in Arizona, where it already had a mortgage bank, and gained regulators' approval to expand into Missouri. The Edina name was continued and its management team was contracted to remain, so, contrary to rumors in the industry, all of the agents in the Twin Cities remained after the purchase. This indicated employee loyalty to Edina and also suggested Metro's good reputation as the new parent company. Edina Realty added about $200 million to Metro's mortgage originations, and Edina Financial Services, with its title insurance and the closing arm, Equity Title, brought in additional income. With this acquisition, Metro entered 1989 as a diversified company—a savings bank, a mortgage bank, and a real estate firm.

Neal St. Anthony, a writer for the *Minneapolis Star and Tribune*, attributed Metro's progress to Norm's "bread and butter style" in which he "largely avoided the pitfalls of riskier commercial lending and executive ineptitude and greed" that had doomed hundreds of S&Ls in the 1980s. Norm stated that the company had stayed close to its Midwestern roots and tried a "few new things," but Metro's bread and butter was still savings accounts, home lending, and consumer financing. St. Anthony continued, "Jones' humility is surpassed only by savvy and studiousness. He's not the cheerleader type, but he gets the job done." Board member Marcil stated that the people in Fargo and North Dakota were not surprised at all that that happened to Metropolitan. The company expanded through aggressive use of the relaxed banking laws, which it could do, because, unlike many other S&Ls, it was in a sound financial condition. But St. Anthony could not resist quoting a financial analyst who called acquiring the bankrupt Minnesota and Iowa thrifts a steal even though the deal met all the requirements of the federal agency and was open to all bidders.

An allusion was made to the fact that Norm had made $213,659 in a recent year, which was called "small potatoes compared to what many banking big shots paid themselves to run smaller or faltering institutions." The article pointed out that the five top executives of the failed First Financial Savings Bank of Des Moines, which was much smaller than Metro, were paid $750,000; plus another $100,000 was spent on expensive automobiles for personal use. Metro's culture would not have tolerated a Cadillac or a Lincoln. Norm stated that the company had a propeller-driven Piper Cherokee, which was not used to ferry executives; many of the Midwest offices were not well served by commercial airlines so a small plane was necessary to get to them. For a company the size of the Des Moines bank, he could understand why it was going broke. "As soon as a greed mentality takes over . . . you see the downward trend of these companies."

The easygoing Norm was driven by faith and business. Associates said, "He is devoutly but quietly religious. He demands from employees strong convictions about ethics. His faith gave him strength when Maurice, twenty years his junior, died of cancer in 1987 at age 37." That event had a major impact on the direction of the company; Norm added that it was no longer a family business since he owned only 2 percent of the stock.

Judging from comments about excessive salaries and perks, it is clear that Norm obviously was bothered by the way many S&Ls conducted their business. He learned that some firms had made loans without inspecting the properties. He commented that one of the first things he had had drilled into him by his grandfather and his father was to always look at the property and never rely on others.

Deregulation allowed S&Ls to compete for funds on the higher yielding money market and to make loans in the more risky commercial markets, all of which provided big opportunities and at the same time greater risks. Bill Nilles added that Metro structured its acquisitions in such a way that they did not negatively impact its reserves, and they stayed in the Midwest where the economy was stronger. Norm cited a case where the company had made a loan on a large office building and "got burned" when the anchor tenant, a bank, went broke. "We lost a little money [but] we revised that real soon."

Metro leadership understood the merger scenario in 1982, but they did not anticipate that so many would lose their entire net worth. This was at a time when industry leaders predicted that of the 3,400 thrifts in 1984, only 2,000 would be left at the end of the 1980s. This is why Metro converted to a stock company because the leadership felt strongly that the public would be impressed about it being a federal bank. Because of all the failures in the industry, Metro had felt it should convert to a federal bank and then become a public company. Their assumption was correct, for deposits increased after they went public and raised money so it could proceed with acquisitions. Norm said, "We decided to pick and choose the businesses that were best for our company. But if you stay too conservative, you'll not make a profit."

There was both external and internal criticism about acquiring Rothschild Mortgage and Edina Realty to diversify geographically and vertically to aid in expanding. Those who looked at the acquisitions strictly from a banker's viewpoint were hesitant, while Norm was more entrepreneurial and looked at the potential for growth. Analysts approved of the acquisitions and noted that earnings prospects were well above average. Their concern about the Edina Realty purchase was that it was too focused on housing, which they felt was too sensitive to recessions and rising interest rates. This was contrary to what the family had always advocated. They pointed out that Metro management had little experience in that segment of the business, to which Norm stated that that was why the Edina management was secured in the deal by having part of their purchase price extended over a three-year period.

Metro wanted to raise capital and at the advice of the investment banking community, it turned to issuing convertible preferred stock. On August 3, 1989, the company floated a $2 convertible preferred stock, which paid 11.5 percent interest and was convertible to common stock at $19 a share. According to Steve

De Wald, director of accounting and financial reporting, this was at a time when S&Ls were not in good standing with the investing public. In this manner it raised $10 million, which was not what it wanted, but, according to analyst Ben Crabtree, "It was still a positive display of fund-raising capability given the recent attitude toward thrifts." Over $50 million had been raised by three stock offerings at the close of the 1989 stock floatation, and higher net profits had helped the tangible net worth increase from $50 million to $115 million.

Not many new acquisitions were made in 1989, but some key moves strengthened the company. Acquiring a branch at Hudson, Wisconsin, opened that state for further activity. First Realty, Iowa's second largest real estate and brokerage firm, brought in $29 million in real estate sales commissions and $67 million in non-interest earnings. Earnings per share increased substantially, and two company favorites—mortgage loans and FSLIC notes—and other housing-related products made up over 73 percent of assets and reserves, for risk-based capital was 50 percent greater than the FSLIC requirement.

Since 1987 the Minneapolis office had grown from three to eighteen employees to handle corporate matters along with the two Twin City subsidiaries, Metropolitan Financial Mortgage Company and Edina Realty.[1]

Number 47 in the Fortune 500

By 1990 only 2,855 out of over 10,000 thrift institutions survived, of which 2,505 were under the Office of Thrift Supervision and had reported losses of $300 million. The RTC supervised the other 350, which had reported losses of $3.1 billion. This figure came from the Advisory Committee of the FDIC, chaired by Norm. At that point the Office of Thrift Supervision established four groups of thrifts: (1) the well-capitalized and profitable 1,264 firms that had $404 billion in assets; (2) the 620 with $326 billion in assets that were expected to meet new capital standards; (3) the 311 with $149 billion in assets that had poor earnings and low capital; and (4) the 310 with $195 billion in assets and were likely to be transferred to the RTC. But even many in the first group had unsatisfactory ratio of capital to assets and return on assets.

Norm, Barbara Bush, Vice President George H. W. Bush, and Eunice Jones at the vice president's home.

In 1989 the company made its first appearance on the Fortune 500 with a ranking of forty-seventh largest savings institution in the nation. It was also recognized for its stock that had yielded more that 20 percent compounded return, based on reinvested dividends and stock splits, from its initial offering in March 1983 through March 31, 1990.

On January 2, 1990, Metro offered a stock swap to First Federal Savings and Loan Association of Council Bluffs, Iowa, which had $176 million in assets and $10 million in tangible net worth, in addition to eight branches in the state. Then, Metro bid on eight Midwest Federal Branches in out-state Minnesota but only acquired one of them and failed in its bid of $3.2 billion for First Minnesota.

However, all was not negative, for in 1990 Metro conducted a major restructuring to enhance its operations. This improved core earnings, and the net increased 15 percent to $75.7 million, making the company the second best performing savings institution with assets over $4 billion, according to *U.S. Banker Magazine*. Deposits increased when the banking offices that previously had been located in Kmart stores were moved to Edina Realty offices and expanded to full financial services. For the second consecutive year, Metro was again on the Fortune 500; the June issue of *Fortune* listed Metro as the twenty-fourth largest savings institution in the nation, up twenty-three places from 1989. For the second year it was in the top ten of all large savings institutions for return on assets, return on equity, and total profitability. In 1990 it was the only institution of the top twenty-five largest that managed to increase its asset size and its total net worth. This followed a long-term company policy that growth has to be fueled by earnings and supported by a strong tangible net worth. MFB, the company's savings bank, had exceeded all current and phased-in regulatory capital requirements established by the "tightened federal standards for the thrift industry."

Unlike the status of those listed in the opening paragraph of this topic, Metro's deposits grew 25 percent in 1990 to $3.4 billion, which included $400 million from RTC for taking over failing thrifts and over $170 million by acquiring First Federal of Council Bluffs, Iowa. Metro became the largest financial institution in North Dakota. It had the most extensive branch network in Minnesota, was the largest thrift company in Iowa, and was the largest thrift with full-service operations in South Dakota and Wisconsin. Bill Bartkowski, senior vice president of corporate relations, commented that no other financial institution operating in the Midwest was as widely owned by individuals living within the region as Metro. More than 80 percent of Metro's shareholders of record lived in North Dakota, Minnesota, Iowa, South Dakota, and Wisconsin. At this point MFB operated 100 banks in ninety-two communities in the six states.

The commitment to North Dakota was strengthened with the acquisition of $400 million in deposits from the acquired thrifts mentioned above that were placed in "strong dynamic markets located throughout the state." In September Metro announced that it was the lowest bidder (i.e. winning bidder), which meant that the FDIC would have to provide the least amount of capital funds to cover potential losses. This deal covered twelve branch offices of Midwest Federal Savings Bank of Minot and two offices of First Savings Association, formerly First Federal of Bismarck, which were insolvent and under control of the RTC.

After the 1989 stock floatation and its continued sound operation policies, Metro was less dependent on government takeover subsidies and one-time gains. In the first nine months of 1990, Metro had paid only $153,000 in taxes on profits of $15.8 million "because of the terms of its 1988 take-over deals." Steve DeWald, corporate controller and chief accounting officer, credited Metro's advantages to being larger than most S&Ls and being able to pick its own mortgage lending while small thrifts had to get into pools to make investments. Metro was able to manage its own portfolio and could grow with the use of increased capital from investments.

The company had grown rapidly since 1988, and management was faced with three major challenges. It was time for restructuring. The first was an emotional decision because of their loyalty to Fargo, but management and the board decided that for better exposure to the financial world, the corporate headquarters of the holding company, MFC, should be moved to Minneapolis. The Fargo loyalists were appeased when it was reaffirmed that the headquarters of MFB would remain in Fargo.

The second was financial. Even though many positive events had taken place in the Midwest during the first nine months of the year, there were still problems in the industry. Paul Lepitzky, president and COO of MFC, stated that in the first nine months of 1990 the company had endured $64.3 million in slow loans compared to $38.8 million in all of 1989. Most of that increase had come from two Arizona and western North Dakota projects that dated back to the early 1980s. Bartkowski thought that that was why MFC had decided in 1988 to exit from the commercial lending business, but the problem lingered.

The third challenge called for a major reorganization in the management staff. During the acquisitions and mergers, Metro had acquired many capable middle management people who no longer fit into the corporate strategy; 115 managerial-level individuals were given generous severance packages. Metro had no obligation to many of these people because they had never been employees of the company. The annual savings was $4 million, of which $1 million came from shedding some top executives.

In some respects Norm set the mode for what took place because he decided that it was time for him to shed some responsibilities of the leadership role. He had pushed himself very hard while building Metro, in addition to maintaining his national connections in the industry. He was sixty years old and wanted to reduce the stress on himself. On October 23, 1990, a five-person executive board was created and called the Office of the Chairman. Norm was relieved of the strain of day-to-day decision making, but he remained well informed of operations by serving as chair of the committee. He was looking for a successor and hopefully that person would come from the committee. The other members of the group included: Paul A. Lipetzky; Stan K. Dardis, CEO of MFB; William P. Bartkowski, chief administrative officer; and Roger L. Rovick, president of Edina Realty.

Norm's stepping down created the usual speculation about what might be next for the company. The company had become known for its aggressive acquisition strategy, but "now the architect of that expansion [had] stepped down as president, and analysts were suggesting that the growth spurt may be over." For the first time since 1926, there was not a Jones active in daily operations, but Norm was still chairman of the board. Rumors quickly spread that the $4.2 billion holding company was on the block. Others watched closely for signs that Metro's magic might have been evaporating. Some expressed amazement. Steven Schroll, analyst for Piper Jaffray & Hopwood, commented, "Jones is one of the most connected people in the S&L industry. He knows who is coming up for bids. . . . He's well connected and savvy politically." Lipetzky told the press that the company would remain the same opportunistic company, but others speculated that his job was to sell it.

Despite all the speculation, the year ended with another honor for Norm when the Center for Innovation and Business Development at the University of North Dakota named him the 1990 North Dakota Business Innovator of the Year. His hometown was proud of a native son who had made his mark on society and especially in his home state. He had created the first North Dakota business to be listed on the New York Stock Exchange and the first North Dakota firm to be included on the *Fortune 500* list.[2]

Mark A. Jones and Metropolitan Financial Services

On January 1, 1991, Bob Clark and many other employees from Fargo were moved to Edina to work in Metro's office there. Clark and most of his fellow Fargoans were "not too happy to move, but they wanted to keep their job with Metro." Unlike the Fargoans who did not want to move to the Twin Cities, Mark A. Jones and his wife, who lived in Phoenix, were happy to be offered a position with Metro and have a chance to live there, because they were not impressed with the Arizona school system and their first child was ready for school. Mark, the third child and first son of Norm and Eunice, stated that in his youth he would sit in his dad's chair and spend time in the community room where the pop machine was. Sometimes he accompanied Norm when he made appraisals and later went on hunting trips, which were often done in conjunction with his father's visits to branch offices. But other than that, he had no connection with the business and his parents did not encourage him to become involved. He remembered that two ladies who were his babysitters told him that some day he would be president of the company.

It was not until after he took a course at North Dakota State School of Science (NDSSS) and then did a summer co-op study with the Metro Insurance Agency that he felt a part of a real team. "I could work with my dad's company but not directly under him. I really enjoyed interacting with the people." After he completed his program at NDSSS, he finished college at Arizona State University (ASU). Then, he took a position with Employers Mutual in Phoenix. He had been advised by Dave Rostad and Dick Horst, who ran the insurance division, that the best way to learn the business was by being in it. After a couple of years, he and a friend thought they wanted to buy a business "but something did not feel right." He called on his professors at ASU to help him with a plan for opening an agency.

The business did well, but then Bill Bartkowski offered him a chance in Metro to do what he had been doing. He started at Metro in Minneapolis in August 1991 working on credit and mortgage insurance for banks, which meant renegotiating new insurance contracts with the banks. This was during a period when the financial services industry was experiencing another wave of deregulation, which presented an opportunity to develop new programs to offer mutual funds, annuities, and life insurance products. Mark was named vice president of non-traditional products and president of MFC's newly created insurance subsidiary, Metropolitan Financial Services. The division quickly

Mark A. Jones, son of Norm and Eunice, joined Metro in August 1991 after several years at an insurance agency. He was largely responsible for establishing Metropolitan Financial Annuity Services.

became a significant contributor to the company's fee income and customer service offerings. Mark had been well trained in the business before coming to Metro and was off to a good start.

During 1991 the company reached an agreement with RTC in which it prepaid a $366 million note issued in 1988. Metro was paid $50 million. In return Metro agreed to forego the use of certain tax benefits. During 1991 the company also sold mortgage-backed securities that yielded a profit of over $30 million, which reduced the risk of holding those mortgages. The negative rate gap experienced during the year reduced to 9.1 percent from 14.9 percent. The historic banking tables show that from January 1 to December 31, 1991, the prime rate dropped from 10 percent to 6.5 percent, which meant that Metro out-performed the average by a considerable degree. Bartkowski pointed out that in the first nine months of 1991, Metro had the strongest core operating income in the history of the company. Since 1988 the tangible capital-to-asset ratio had increased from 1.8 percent, to 3.07 percent in 1989, to 3.54 percent in 1990, to 4.1 percent in 1991. That ratio surpassed all FIRREA-mandated levels causing one industry expert to state the MFC's growth of capital was "one of the best ongoing success stories in the industry." At year's end Metro still had $180 million in operating loss carry-forwards to offset future tax liability, but with all of the positives it became the upper Midwest's largest and best capitalized saving institution. MFC had 125 savings banks located in 101 communities in six states. It was the largest originator of residential mortgage loans in the Twin Cities and western Wisconsin where Edina Realty had thirty-five offices and over 1,600 sales representatives. Metro financed over 40 percent of the 15,000 to 20,000 homes Edina sold annually, and Equity Title Service, Inc., which was also a subsidiary, was the largest title company in Minnesota.

The strong Metropolitan culture helped it to increase market share in over half of the communities it served. It was able to retain customers and increase the vast majority of deposits and firms it had acquired since 1988 from the FSLIC and RTC despite the challenges of branch office consolidation and ongoing systems integration. In late 1991 it was approached by the RTC to take over Security Financial Group, Inc., which, with its nine branches, was the fourth largest Minnesota-based S&L. The federal regulators had "lambasted [Security's] management for a loss-plagued commercial real estate portfolio that wiped out earnings in 1990 and 1991 and had $11 million in non-performing assets." When the deal took place on February 28, 1992, Security and its nine branches had $260 million in assets. Metro acquired them for $12.8 million in MFC common stock.

During 1991 net operating income before loss provisions rose 39 percent for the third record-breaking year to $105 million; non-interest income was $84 million; and net assets climbed to $4.67 billion. All of the above led to healthy gains for the stockholders who received a 15 percent cash dividend in January, 5 percent in October plus a 2-for-1 stock dividend, and another 10 percent cash dividend for January 1992. Cash dividends had increased annually since 1985, "a record unmatched in our industry."

After Metro purchased American Charter of Lincoln, Nebraska, Mark learned that it offered annuities and mutual funds. He met with American's people in charge of that service and found out that it was a profitable business, but Metro had tried twice before to do brokerage business and withdrew both times. It became Mark's job to sell the board on the idea of reentering that activity, and they were convinced that it was the wave of the future. Then, he had to get approval from the Office of Thrift Approval to proceed. He studied American's procedure, and within a year Metro had forty-eight representatives in nine states. By 1993 the program generated $2.8 million in revenue, and the next year it made $4.3 million. Little did anyone realize at the time, but the financial services program melded well into First Bank's plans, which would later buy Metro.[3]

Norman Jones, Chair of SAIFIAC

On July 2, 1992, Norm, as head of Savings Association Insurance Fund Industry's Advisory Committee on the Adequacy of the Savings Association Insurance Fund (SAIFIAC), which was created by an act of Congress, issued a detailed account to the FDIC and Congress about the desperate shortage in the insurance fund to cover the failures that still were forthcoming. The report appealed for an extension on the deadline for the RTC to continue to meet the obligations. The RTC was designed to complete, in an orderly fashion, its job of resolving those institutions that could not return to health and to provide the Savings Association Insurance Fund (SAIF) time to build its fund balances. Norm's committee realized that the S&L crisis was far from over. The RTC Improvement Act of 1991 provided that beginning in fiscal year 1997, the Treasury was to make annual payments to SAIF an amount equal to the difference between the premiums deposited into SAIF and $2 billion needed to build the fund and additional payments to keep the minimum levels specified by law.

The SAIFIAC report stated, "Certainly no one wants to experience another deposit insurance emergency crisis, or permit failing institutions to languish and build even greater ultimate losses because inadequate funds exist to resolve them or read reports of an insolvent SAIF." The committee realized that there was only $153 million in the SAIF balance, and it foresaw

157

insurance obligations of $1.453 billion by September 30, 1993. That meant the Treasury would have to contribute at least another $1 billion during 1992. To raise premium levels on exiting S&Ls would only place a greater burden on the surviving institutions. This was why Norm's committee was appealing for more help. The problem was further exacerbated because there was no evidence that public confidence in the surviving institutions had improved by what RTC had done with public funds. "The surviving SAIF-insured institutions continue to be frustrated by the taint of the sins of long-gone institutions to which the survivors bear no relationship or resemblance. But they are even more frustrated by the requirement that they continue to pay for losses for which they bear no responsibility, which, to the fund that insures their deposits, receives no benefit from the assessments they pay." The surviving S&Ls felt that they should be paying only to current operations.

The SAIFIAC members knew that there were 110 institutions with $88 billion in aggregate assets that were slated for seizure, and the total potential problem was still underestimated. In addition, there were many other S&Ls that were "critically undercapitalized" and would have to be placed in receivership. The committee did not believe the RTC could save the bottom 20 percent of critically undercapitalized thrifts representing $10 billion in assets, and it believed they would fail by September 30, 1993. The greatest danger was that the 165 undercapitalized institutions with a net worth of 2 to 4 percent and a combined total assets of $106 billion possibly could not survive longer than 1993. However, they were at risk because of the uncertain economy and declining real estate values. Another 159 thrifts with assets of $66 billion and a tangible net worth averaging 5.06 percent were "marginally undercapitalized" and would not meet FIRREA requirements by the end of 1994. They probably would need as much as $22 billion. Maybe a "holding pen" would be required for the seized thrifts but this would "not be a way of instilling confidence in the SAIF and in surviving institutions."

The report closed: "The Jones-led SAIF committee was appealing to the FDIC, the Office of Management and Budget (OMB), Treasury, and Congress to determine the amount of shortfall and make up the difference." It forecasted that SAIF would receive a shortfall from Treasury funding of at least $1.84 billion or higher, depending "on the timing of failures" and when payments were made. The FDIC estimated that there would be failures ranging from $50 billion to $250 billion over the next four years.[4]

Surge and Purge

Rod Jordahl related that when the company was growing quickly, it went through a surge and purge period. Nearly every thrift had one or two top-notch people who had potential to fit into a larger company, but there were always a few who had to be let out. Until he was stricken with cancer and died in December 1987, Morrie Jones was assumed to be the heir apparent. In early 1988 Paul Lipetzky, a seventeen-year employee of Metro's external auditor Ernst and Whinney, was hired as chief financial officer of MFC. Lipetzky was very focused and driven, and even though he had worked as an independent auditor for several years on Metro's books, "he did not look into the company's heritage and he brought in many outsiders." Metro employees who worked with the Ernst and Whinney firm knew that Lipetzky was not well liked by his colleagues there, but he worked well with the top echelon. There was no question that he was an excellent CPA—he was sharp and decisive, but he was not a people person. This was in contrast to Norm and Bill Nilles, who generally were liked by everyone, which was a key to the company's success. One board member stated, "Lipetzky was so talented, but he did not have the personality to adapt to Metropolitan's culture. He could not develop a good relationship with people who worked under him and/or with him."

Steve DeWald was an accountant at Ernst and Whinney before he joined Metro, so he knew Lipetzky. DeWald said, "He was quiet, very sharp, very deliberate, and direct in his dealings. He had an accountant-like personality but was a very good administrator." Board member Marcil, who was well versed in the corporate world, commented, "Lipetzky was not of our culture and just did not fit in with Metropolitan's thinking. But in his defense, when he was employed, there was a job for him to do." Gary Dietz, a middle level manager, understood what the job was, for he was one of the 115 management people who were discharged at that fateful time in late October 1990. Dietz, who had a good career with Metro and understood what was taking place, felt everyone was well treated by the company despite the early exodus. "He [Lipetzky] did not fit in the Metro culture. He was arrogant and not well liked but was a good hatchet man."

Norm commented that he created the five-person board to find a successor. Bartkowski surmised that "Norm . . . was thoughtful, humble, and low key, and I think fully intended to sit back, but when he saw Paul's explosiveness, he decided it would not work." There were some potential acquisitions that Lipetzky could not close, which bothered the board and Norm. He said, "We were still doing lots of acquisitions and the sellers always wanted to talk to me, so my load was not reduced."

At another meeting, shortly after Norm came back, the board realized that some delegated changes had not been made. Board member Larsen spoke up and said that nothing had changed. "Paul was furious, and after the meeting he challenged me firsthand. He was so mad because I had compared him to Rothschild. This really upset Lipetzky because he could see the future. He could not stand anyone disputing his opinions."

In July 1992, after twenty-one months out of the driver's seat, Norm decided to return as chief executive. The December 1992 issue of *Corporate Report Minnesota* gave an extensive account of the events in an article entitled "Error Apparent: Paul Lipetzky Thought He Would Be Running Metropolitan Financial, Norman Jones Had Another Idea." By this time Metro had quietly become a large company with $6.6 billion in assets and offices in 180 locations in six states, and had surpassed Twin City Federal. The company had grown and was profitable during the twenty-one months that Norm was not in charge. Norm felt that there were many opportunities ahead for acquisitions. He said, "The board felt and I felt that with all my experience in the past forty years it would be easier . . . [to grow] if I was the day-to-day CEO rather that just the chair. You can't put that task down. . . . They want to talk to the CEO."

Board member Laurence Davis, retired Edina Realty executive, commented that he was hopeful that Lipetzky would remain: "Norman, the great generator and creator of opportunities as CEO and Paul [Lipetzky] an outstanding administrator." Norm had told Lipetzky that he wanted him to remain to lead operations as president. But Lipetzky was not willing to do so and resigned in August 1992. Norm was sixty-two and mentioned his friend Carl Pohlad, who at age seventy-seven was still directing his company. Norm "saw an opportunity for Metro to become one of the top four or five thrifts in the nation and confessed he would like to be a part of that."

Metro had acquired many good managers to select from to get the job done. Bartkowski, Stan Dardis, and Norm shared some of Lipetzky's work, and Steve DeWald was named chief financial officer. A close friend of Norm, but not in the company, commented that employing Lipetzky was probably Norm's only mistake in selecting top leaders, but maybe he was the right person when taken aboard. Eunice commented that the Lipetzky affair was difficult because of the way the media handled it.[5]

Norm, the Deal Maker

In 1992, *Fortune* ranked MFC the nineteenth largest savings institution in the nation and listed its stock as one of the fifty best performing on the NYSE for 1991. It was the thirty-third best performing firm in market appreciation in excess of 175 percent and the best performing thrift institution on the "big board." After the brief semi-retirement, Norm returned to continue his acquisition program. Even though Tony Carideo, a columnist for the *Minneapolis Star and Tribune*, could not resist making a cute remark that Norm remained retired long enough to earn a $1.8-million retirement benefit, Norm's fellow leaders in the industry were happy to see him back. The analysts were obviously more comfortable because they understood his leadership ability. Norm commented that the analysts did not know very well the eight of the top twenty-six people that the company had gained through acquisitions. He added that these were the people who had given Metro a good track record that enabled it to avoid the pitfalls that some of the big firms like Twin City Federal were caught in.

One reporter recalled that when Norm stepped down in 1990, the rumor mill had it that Metro was on the block and it was Lipetzky's mission to sell the company. Those who knew better stated that acquisitions would be made as the opportunities came along. Norm added that he felt he had to return to seize the opportunity for more acquisitions and threw out the suggestion that Metro was on track to grow assets to $10 billion in three years. Those who were close to Norm realized that he missed the action.

He said, "Throughout the last fifteen years, I've kind of been the architect of mergers and acquisitions and it's a people business. He [Lipetzky] did not know the people as well as I do after forty years in the business." Even though Metro had done well in his absence, it had a slower growth after several years of surging ahead and experiencing some big tax breaks because of those deals. But future earnings would be dependent on a future acquisition strategy and high margin consumer loans to build on its solid base.

Much of Metro's growth had come about because of poor decisions made by previous failed S&L managers. Bartkowski recalled that it had acquired fourteen sick but curable institutions as federal regulators sold them off. "They were very good deals, but there was risk involved and we worked very hard on them. We invested $40 million in capital to revive them." To which Norm added that they were fortunate in disposing of the thrift's problem assets, which were mostly non-producing real estate loans.

Charles Crabtree, analyst for Dain Bosworth, knew well how Metro worked. It was conservative in its operations while pursuing an aggressive but well-calculated acquisition strategy. Norm continued to adhere to his father's method of operation, but he used his own instincts on how to acquire, which was not the elder's forte. On another occasion Crabtree felt that Metro would make more acquisitions.

> These guys [Metro] are the most aggressive and adept acquirers. . . . While believing that they'll be making acquisitions is a bit of an article of faith . . . he's willing to take that gamble. You have to recognize that over the last ten years this is a company that has had a great number of opportunities to do many stupid things. But it didn't.

Bill Brouse, president of the Wisconsin League of Financial Institutions, who had known Norm for thirty years, said, "He really knows the industry's problems and challenges. He has been a regular on the scene in Washington for the last twenty-five years. He has lots of street and business smarts, and younger troops look to him as a mentor in addition to being a leader." To this, Dick Buendorf, the Minnesota League's president, injected, "Jones had the kind of personality that generates trust. He's a very gentle executive and very likeable. He's not someone who lets success go to his head. He's not pompous, overbearing, or dictatorial." Brouse continued, "Norm had a plan in mind since his days in Fargo."

When asked about his plan, Norm added that it was to stick to the Midwest market where the economy is stable and the people pay their bills, and to remember that the basic business of thrifts is to help people buy homes and save money. He continued,

> We stayed true to our mission. A lot of companies, not just banks and thrifts, haven't. A few years ago the vogue . . . was to try to get into something not related to your business. Most major companies have not done well at that. We have tried other things once in a while, but there was never a large risk involved.

Norm understood and openly acknowledged that his relationships in the industry gave Metro an edge in making deals. He was on five federal boards, which put him in touch with the inner workings of the industry and in a position to advise what could be done to correct the problems. Much of his influence came about because of his personality and the fact that people liked and trusted him.

In the second quarter of 1992, there was some concern by the regulators because Metro had assembled about $1 billion in fixed-rate mortgages but then it sold $919 million in mortgages and made a $44.3 million gain. It had addressed three major concerns of analysts—credit risk, interest rate risk, and capital levels. After that Norm was poised to move ahead. A third quarter subordinated note offering—notes given by the company which paid a higher-than-market rate of interest but were subordinate to all secured creditors—generated $87.25 million. The ability to raise this amount of money indicated tremendous faith in the company management. In addition, MFB had record core earnings, which qualified the company as being well capitalized under the regulators' standards. This meant that Norm was quite sure he would have the go ahead on National City and Western in Kansas. He was convinced his team could handle the "challenges in handling the growing multi-state franchise and getting a higher value for its [Metro's] stock."

During 1992 Monycor Savings of Barron, Wisconsin, with deposits of $73 million was purchased. That was followed by First Federal of Rapid City, South Dakota, with deposits of $160 million, and Security Financial of St. Cloud, which had assets of $220 million and deposits of $200 million. Then, American Charter of Lincoln, Nebraska, was acquired. American had $947 million in assets and $853 million in deposits. That purchase was followed by the acquisition of Homeowners Federal of Fergus Falls, with $134 million in assets and $117 in deposits.

The stock writers and analysts were all agog by the way Norm was able to consummate deals so rapidly. Steve Schroll of Piper Jaffray called Norm "a deal maker who has proved he's good at it time and time again," to which Norm replied, "We had tremendous opportunities for mergers, and I thought we'd get them accomplished a little better if I was back as the CEO. Mergers are a very personal thing. People are selling their companies and I know those people."

By late 1992 the company had "widened its lending margins and expanded its real estate and mortgage banking arms," which increased its earnings. At the same time it had big gains in security sales and realized tax benefits via the subsidized purchases of S&Ls from the government. Analyst Kinnard Eaynes said of Metropolitan, "Historically, it's a very savvy management that seemed to take appropriate action ahead of industry changes," and it had the capital to expand. Norm responded to the above remarks: "We foresee in the next few years being a $10 billion company. We don't have to take a lot away from the major players to do that."

In November 1992 *The Business Journal* reported that Metro was making plans to buy Western Financial Corporation of Overland Park, Kansas, and its subsidiary Columbia Savings Association, with its twenty-four savings banks in the state. Western was a $665 million publicly held thrift, which the company could purchase with capital it gained from acquiring National City, and it would give Metro strong inroads into Kansas. *The Journal* article stated that Western "was loaded with potential problems" because of a low equity-to-asset ratio and 105 percent non-performing loans. It had lost $8.6 million in the two previous years, and the regulators mandated an increase in loan loss reserves, which placed it under the supervision of the Office of Thrift

Supervision. Analysts were all speculating on how good or bad Western might be for Metro.

At the close of 1992, Metro had $6.1 billion in assets. During 1992 it had closed on seven deals with assets of $2.5 billion in assets and $2.2 billion in deposits, totaling twenty-seven financial institutions acquired since 1982. Those institutions had 200 offices located in seven states and plans called for continued growth. Norm commented, "We have sure been the shark, more than shark bait." During the first nine months, it had a return of 1.48 percent on assets and a 20.7 percent return on equity before extraordinary items and accounting changes, well above industry standards.

The annual report for 1992 stated that on August 26, the top twenty-six managers assembled to plan the road ahead: have $10 billion in assets by 1995 without sacrificing credit quality; acquire companies compatible with MFC's culture; and improve consumer lives and help them attain financial and home ownership goals. It was management's opinion that to compete effectively for capital, the institution would have to reach $10 billion in assets in the next eighteen to thirty-six months. To reach that goal MFC would have to extend beyond its seven states. Its decision was that "America's Heartland is a strong market and a market we know and have served for nearly seventy years. Our present plans will not take us outside these markets." The reason was based on the consensus that Metro had less competition for deposits because "most of our bank branches are located in areas where our competitors are small, locally owned banks." MFC's size and product offering gave it great advantage, so it had a stable and relatively low-cost source of funds. Also, Edina Realty gave it a competitive advantage in the Twin Cities.

The discussion continued with short-term goals of "aggressively seeking [purchasing opportunities] with emphasis on in-market acquisitions and plans to become more efficient, reduce expenses, and increase productivity." The other goals were to "stay independent, advance shareholder value, promote thrift and home ownership, and focus on the Heartland." Even though Norm spent most of his time out-of-state, he was not forgotten by his North Dakota friends, and in October 1992 the Greater North Dakota Association—the State Chamber of Commerce—presented him with The Greater North Dakotan Award.[6]

The Competition Becomes Keener

Following the August 1992 board meeting, the company fine tuned its management procedures and closed seventeen branches and laid off 100 employees to become more competitive against the stronger and larger remaining thrifts. There were still troubled thrifts available for acquisition, but because of competition they commanded premium prices. As Norm became more involved, it became clear to Stanley Dardis, one of the top officers, that Norm would not be retiring in the near future, so he resigned. This again created a wave of speculation "about succession, or the lack of it . . . as well as about such things as the company's ability to acquire and digest new banking properties." It was one columnist's opinion that the management structure was clearly designed to keep anyone from rising to the number two spot. Others speculated about future mergers or divestitures, but none knew what Norm had in mind.

Metro had reduced its non-performing loans to a minimum, and its non-interest expenses were down because of increased efficiencies, but the analysts had concerns about the large non-performing assets of Western Financial. Norm ignored that talk, and while in Omaha to play golf at the Warren Buffett Benefit Gold Tournament for a children's theater, he spoke to the press about the great potential in Iowa and Nebraska. He repeated a favorite theme, "We call this the heartland of our nation, the area where people still have values, pay their bills, and save a fair amount." He added that the Midwest economy remained stable and neither inflation nor economic downturns tend to be very steep.

Was that talk to keep competitors off base? In any case, just a few weeks later the September 1993 issue of the *American Banker* released the news that Metro had purchased Rocky Mountain Financial Corporation, the parent company of a Cheyenne-based savings bank, with $559 million in assets for $64.2 million in cash. This was Wyoming's second largest financial institution. It increased MFC's assets to about $7.6 billion, and its fourteen branches gave Metro a presence in Wyoming and a loan office in Colorado. Unlike many previous acquisitions, Rocky Mountain had an excellent credit quality and solid profitability. Norm said it was strong and well managed and he would retain its management team. The industry perceived this purchase as a springboard into the

Rocky Mountain States, especially Colorado and Montana. Its acquisition had an immediate, positive impact on Metro stock, which was not doing as well as some of its competitors. "As a result, speculation was sparked among some analysts that Metropolitan, itself, could be vulnerable to takeover."

Although the purchase of Rocky Mountain was not closed until March 25, 1994, the opening of negotiations was a turning point in some respects because First Bank System was considering acquiring it, as were others. As stated earlier, consolidation was becoming part of the new environment, which "heated up the bidding as banks rose from one and one-half times book to two times. The good sign was that this meant that the S&L crisis was nearing the end, and the industry was getting back to solid ground."

In his annual report for 1993, Norm wrote that by acquiring Western Financial Corporation of Overland Park with its twenty branches and the Eureka Savings Bank of Eureka, Kansas, and its ten branches, Metro's assets increased by $1 billion. It was also in full negotiations with Rocky Mountain Financial with its fourteen branches.

Total assets increased by over $1 billion, and the return on assets and equity were solid. In addition to the two acquisitions, cash flow was greatly helped by a 30 percent increase in net interest income before provision for loan losses of $198 million and $89.9 million in non-interest income from fees and services. Subsidiary Edina Realty provided $570 million in mortgage loan origination, nearly 35 percent of MFC's new loan production. It also generated $35.3 million in commissions and $13.7 million in title closing fees. Metropolitan Financial Services added Liberty Securities Corporation, a registered broker-dealer, to help bank customers with financial advice and fixed and variable annuities, mutual funds, unit investment trusts, and life insurance.

Mortgage loans, the traditional bread-and-butter earner, increased from 9,876 in 1992 to 15,975 in 1993, and the total value of those loans rose from $974 million to $1.3 billion. *The Fortune 500* listed Metro for the second time and ranked it the twelfth largest savings institution and recognized it as the leader of thrifts over $5 billion in all segments. All of the above was good news for the stockholders, who, in addition to good dividends, realized a two-to-one stock split at year's end.[7]

Putting A Ribbon on the Package

On March 11, 1994, Norman M. Jones received the *Financial World's* Bronze Award as one of the thrift industries three best executives. He was a two-time winner of the award; his first was in 1987. This award came in part because he had served as chairman of the Savings Association Insurance Fund Industry Advisory Committee. His election to that position came about because he was recognized for his keen insights on the savings industry. The *American Banker* did a feature article on Norm later, and in response he received letters of congratulations from industry leaders throughout the nation that reflected their respect of his sincerity, trustworthiness, and solid leadership. The article related how since 1984 he had led Metro in acquiring twenty-eight institutions with 211 branches controlling $7.8 billion in assets making it the eleventh largest thrift holding company in the nation. States, in order of number of offices, were: Minnesota, 58; North Dakota, 33; Iowa, 31; Kansas, 31; Missouri, 26; Wyoming, 14; South Dakota, 10; Ohio, 6; Wisconsin, 6; and Arizona, 2. In 1993 it had a return on assets of 0.98 percent and a 14 percent return on average equity.

Ben Crabtree, a prominent banking analyst for Dain Bosworth in the Twin Cities, said, "You'd be hard-pressed to find a company that has taken better advantage of the problems in the thrift industry. They have been great acquirers." Crabtree said that Jones was a down-to-earth manager and one of the industry's shrewdest acquirers. Bartkowski commented that it was really "Norm's vision and his leadership that made the company what it is." He added that Metropolitan's "corporate culture is infected with Mr. Jones' near-insatiable desire to grow." Bartkowski recalled the excitement one day in 1988 when six insolvent thrifts were acquired, and Metro's assets and deposits doubled that afternoon. Norm's reply to that comment was, "Companies that are stagnant and do not grow are generally not very good investments."

Prior to 1994 Norm was considering acquiring banks, but the rising price for bank stock caused him to change his plans, and for the first time in years the company had no purchases pending. There was speculation about why Norm "was not making any preparation for succession, which is generally thought of as a primary responsibility. [His] inaction made some observers 'uncomfortable.' Others say it may be a sign that Metropolitan, the ultimate acquirer, is itself now ready to be taken over." The article

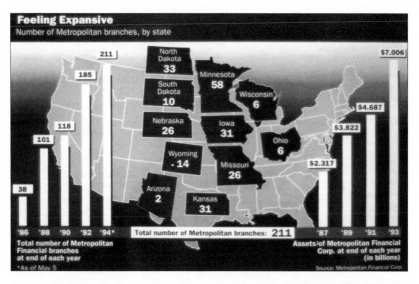

Feeling Expansive
Number of Metropolitan branches, by state

211

185

118

101

38

'86 '88 '90 '92 '94*

Total number of Metropolitan
Financial branches
at end of each year
*As of May 5

North Dakota 33

South Dakota 10

Nebraska 26

Wyoming -14

Arizona 2

Minnesota 58

Wisconsin 6

Iowa 31

Missouri 26

Kansas 31

Ohio 6

Total number of Metropolitan branches: 211

$7.006

$4.687

$3.822

$2.317

'87 '89 '91 '93

Assets of Metropolitan Financial
Corp. at end of each year
(in billions)

Source: Metropolitan Financial Corp.

Assets, location, and number of branches before the final acquisitions in 1994. Photo credit American Banker.

continued saying that Norm was not concerned and that there never really was an heir apparent. His view of the world was "you either go ahead or you fall back" and he was prepared for anything. He closed the interview, "In the next five years, you're going to see major consolidations. We hope we can put together enough deals so that we're the long-term survivor." On May 1, 1994, over 100 employees who had occupied offices in the Twin Cities since 1991 were moved into three floors of what was formerly called the Lincoln Centre and now re-named the Metropolitan Centre. Only a few weeks earlier these floors had not been touched beyond the exterior walls, so everything was completely new.

After Rocky Mountain was acquired for a fairly good premium, Bartkowski recalled that Trueman Tryhus asked if Metro would sell for that kind of a premium. Norm responded, "Would anyone pay it?" Soon after Norm walked across the street and asked Richard Zona, now the chief financial officer at First Bank and with whom Norm had a close relationship, if he would pay that much. Steve DeWald said that the purchase of Rocky Mountain "slowed down our opportunities." Tryhus commented that Norm was showing signs of stress, and "I think maybe Rick Zona might have planted the idea that First Bank would be a potential buyer."

In August 1988, Metropolitan Financial opened its corporate office in the Lincoln Center at 333 South Seventh Street in Minneapolis. In July 1993, when Metropolitan announced that it would be moving most of its Twin City personnel to the centre, it became the major tenant and the building was renamed Metropolitan Centre.

Bartkowski related his favorite story about Norm:

After it was decided to sell the company, one day Norm came into my office after he had a meeting with Jack Grundhoffer, the president of First Bank, and shut the door. Norm was so bothered by the rough talk and was confused by it because he knew Grundhoffer was active in his church. Norm did not like shady stories. He was such a gentleman.

Norm was asked when the thought of selling had first come to him. He stated that it was in July 1993 when Bill Cooper, president of Twin City Federal, proposed a merger with them. The chemistry was not right. But about six months prior to that Jack Grundhoffer and Rick Zona had coffee with Norm and "hinted that they would like to buy whenever I wanted to sell. I knew and liked Zona." Then, Metro called on Dain Bosworth to determine its worth. The Dain data was discussed with the board and the question was, would someone pay the price? It was agreed to find out what First Bank might be willing to pay because "their territory fit our customer base well." Norm continued, "I talked to Zona and they offered $2 a share more than the Dain evaluation, so we sold."

First Bank System Inc. of Minneapolis announced on July 1, 1994, that it intended to buy Metropolitan Financial Corporation. First Bank had $26.5 billion in assets and operated in six states where Metro did business and wanted to expand into Iowa, Kansas, Nebraska, and Wyoming where it did not have branches, so analysts were not surprised by the move. Metropolitan had assets of over $8 billion with $5.6 billion in deposits and served over 500,000 customers. In addition, Metropolitan Financial Services held licenses for forty-nine investment executives and had achieved more than $200 million in investment sales.

Steven Schroll of Piper, an obvious booster of Norm, said of the prospective sale: "In terms of a strategic fit it was almost like hand in glove. . . . [Metropolitan] expanded through a series of acquisitions that cannily exploited the thrift industry's weakened state in the 1980s. . . . It did a great job of putting together a franchise that was bigger and more successful than was imaginable five or ten years ago. But they were not able to attract or develop enough key managers . . . to keep up with the increase in assets and the complexity of managing such a business spread over many states. . . . The buyout agreement was a decision that was better for the shareholders."

METROPOLITAN Locations

Metropolitan Federal Bank

North Dakota	Minnesota			Kansas	Wisconsin
Beach	Aitkin	New Prague	North Platte	Andover	Barron
Beulah	Albert Lea	Ortonville	Ogallala	Augusta	Bloomer
Bismarck	Alexandria	Owatonna	Omaha	Clay Center	Hudson
Bottineau	Blooming Prairie	Pelican Rapids	Seward	Colby	Rice Lake
Cavalier	Blue Earth	Perham	Superior	El Dorado	Spooner
Crosby	Brainerd	Pine City	Valentine	Emporia	
Devils Lake	Brooklyn Center	Pine River	York	Eureka	**Arizona**
Dickinson	Burnsville	Plymouth		Fredonia	Mesa
Ellendale	Chisago City	Princeton	**Iowa**	Gardner	Scottsdale
Fargo	Chisholm	Prior Lake	Ackley	Greensburg	
Garrison	Columbia Heights	Rochester	Altoona	Holton	**Wyoming**
Grafton	Coon Rapids	Saint Cloud	Ankeny	Iola	Casper
Grand Forks	Crosby	Saint Paul	Belmond	Larned	Cheyenne
Jamestown	Eagan	Sauk Centre	Carlisle	Lawrence	Cody
Kenmare	Edina	Sauk Rapids	Charles City	Manhattan	Evanston
Langdon	Elbow Lake	Sleepy Eye	Clarinda	Oberlin	Gillette
Lisbon	Elk River	Starbuck	Clear Lake	Osage City	Green River
Mandan	Fergus Falls	Stillwater	Council Bluffs	Overland Park	Lander
Minot	Gaylord	Wayzata	Creston	Prairie Village	Laramie
Northwood	Grand Rapids	West St. Paul	Des Moines	Pratt	Riverton
Rugby	Granite Falls	Wheaton	Forest City	Topeka	Rock Springs
Stanley	Hibbing		Hampton	Wamego	Sheridan
ValleyCity	Madison	**Nebraska**	Iowa Falls	Wichita	Torrington
Wahpeton	Mankato	Beatrice	Knoxville		Worland
Watford City	Maple Grove	Bellevue	Lake Mills	**South**	
West Fargo	Maplewood	Columbus	Mason City	**Dakota**	Fort Collins,
Williston	Minneapolis	Crete	Missouri Valley	Flandreau	Colorado
	Minnetonka	Fairbury	Northwood	Mitchell	
	Montevideo	Hastings	Osage	Pierre	
	Monticello	Kearney	Pella	Rapid City	
	Moorhead	Lexington	Red Oak	Sioux Falls	
	Mora	Lincoln	West Des Moines	Sturgis	
		McCook			

Chart showing location of the 220 branches at the time of sale, July 1, 1994.

First Bank offered $863 million in stock which meant that Metro shareholders would get between 0.683 and 0.7347 shares of First's stock for each share they had. At the announcement Metro's stock jumped from $15.75 to $21.75 per share. Up to that date it was "the second-largest thrift transaction ever." Trueman Tryhus added, "Selling was like putting a ribbon on the package and presenting it to the shareholders and citizens of North Dakota."[8]

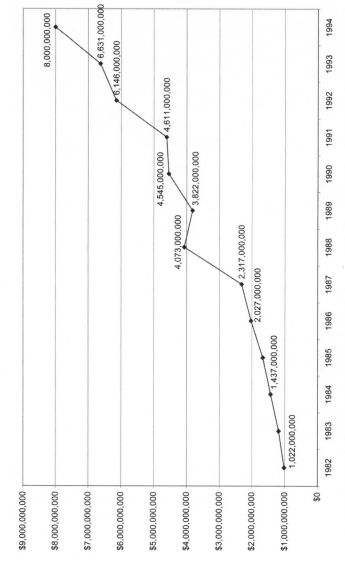

**Assets in Billions of Dollars
1982-1994**

Chart showing growth in assets in billions from 1982 to 1994. Compare with charts on pages 37 and 87.

Norm and Eunice with President George W. Bush.

Going Out on Top

Within days of the announcement that First Bank intended to purchase Metro, calls and letters of joy reached the office. Paul T. Filipi, a stockholder from Omaha, wrote:

> I want to thank you for your leadership . . . that has had a great impact on my life. I am now able to be very generous with charities and my grandchildren. While I am sure you would be the first to credit others for their help, the fact remains YOU were the dominant person in the great success we all enjoy. . . . My wish for you is continued happiness; you got it the old fashioned way. YOU EARNED IT.

Robert J. Aylward from New York wrote: "Dear Norman, As a long-time shareholder in Metropolitan, I would like to congratulate you on a job well done! You have helped to reinforce our value-oriented investment approach."

Eilene Sweet, a Metro employee since 1970 and the first female branch office manager, said that she quit because she so enjoyed her relationship with and working with Norm and Bill Nilles and "knew working with others would be too different and not near the fun."

In the first article in *The Forum* after the sale closed, Norm stated that there was tremendous consolidation in the industry to gain the efficiencies provided by technology and posed the question of how does an $8 billion company compete against a $26.5 billion one? Everyone realized that the stockholders would have a 50 percent increase in share value and severance payments of $9.9 million to many long-time employees. Bill Nilles commented to this writer, "It made me rich." Norm said, "The offer was just too attractive to pass up."

Weeks later *The Forum* wrote that $1,000 invested in 1983 was worth $12,653 on the day of the sale. With accumulated dividends, that was an annualized return of 30 percent.

An employee of fifteen years, whose husband was a maintenance worker, said their $20,250 investment grew to $855,000 when she sold it in 1998. Her husband had encouraged his fellow workers to buy and "they have all thanked him or me whenever we meet." Noel Fedje said that he felt so good about many local people who had previously only purchased CDs but had faith in the Jones family. In 1989 one couple came to him for direction about Metro stock, and he encouraged them to buy $2 convertible preferred that paid 11.5 percent. Their $10,000 investment was worth $79,000 after the sale in 1995. Then, they came to him for more advice. He asked them if they had ever taken a vacation. They had not, so he encouraged them to take one. Fedje, who managed the Fargo office of Dain Bosworth, which had over sixty branches, added that the Metropolitan stock was one the largest and most profitable accounts for the company and the stockholders that Dain ever had. He personally had twenty-eight accounts that netted over a million dollars each on Metro stock.[9]

After Metropolitan

On January 25, 1995, The First Bank System Thrift subsidiary was created; it included many former MFB officers. Most of the Metro employees received positions with First, many of whom joined the First U.S. Bank service center that opened in Fargo and employed about 1,500. Apparently, Norm lobbied behind the scenes to get that center to Fargo. Norm joined the First Bank board and chairman of its trust division to work on mergers and acquisitions. While attending a board meeting in Seattle in February 1998, he suffered a mild heart attack, but, fortunately, it caused no lasting damage. He remained with First Bank until July 1998 and continued to serve on boards of directors for other business corporations and charities.

Mark commented,

> After the sale it was a soul-searching time for me. I had been in a really good position and I also considered buying an insurance firm, but after a few months I got involved in starting Metro Community Bank. Dad felt that it should have at least $2 million capital to be competitive.

In December 1996 Metro Community Bank opened at 510 Marquette Avenue and a branch was opened in the Twin Cities. Norm, Mark, Rod Hanson, and Bev Austin, plus a few stockholders from Fargo, were the founders.

All involved soon learned that a small bank had the same regulations as the larger ones but had fewer people to cope with them. It was much more labor intensive than working in a large bank where everyone had a definite assignment. Mark said, "Everyone agreed that after being used to a big operation it was difficult to adjust to a small ship—the flare was gone!"

The American Banker encouraged banks to sell traditional insurance products so Norm approached Minnesota Mutual Life Insurance Company, which appeared to have an interest, but they did not follow up. Then, Norm contacted Lutheran Brotherhood Insurance Company who knew that Aid Association for Lutherans owned banks. They were interested because they understood the potential that owning banks offered them. In 1998 the bank was sold to Lutheran Brotherhood.

As a parting thought, Mark, who was only seven years younger than his uncle Morrie, commented that if Morrie had lived, he did not think that Metropolitan Financial Corporation would have been sold. "We were really good buddies and we would have gone forward." But his father and the board might have felt otherwise. Mark has continued his career with Trans America in northern California.

During an interview in 1999, when Norm was asked how he would like to have Metro remembered, he said, "For having excellent employees who cared about their work. For helping a great many people become home owners, and for helping many average investors do very, very well." He praised former Metro customers, "They created a wonderful atmosphere for us to operate in. We were very fortunate." The people of North Dakota honored him again in October 2000 when he received the Schafer Excellence in Enterprise Award from the Harold Schafer Leadership Center of the University of Mary in Bismarck. The award was for displaying "outstanding entrepreneurial spirit and respect for others exemplified by the life and career" of Harold Schafer. Friends Eugene and Lila Dahl wrote, "I really think our building the Steiger plant and your [Metro] financing was a turning point in Fargo's industrialization." Noel Fedje added his congratulations: "No one is more deserving of this entrepreneurial award. . . . It amazes me at all the wealth creation that was provided by Metro stock and your leadership."[10]

~   ~   ~   ~   ~

1. Barth, pp. 79, 82, 84; *Supplemental Report to the Second Annual Report of the Industry Advisory Committee*, pp. 13, 15, 28, Norman M. Jones, chairman; Metro Hist. pp. 25, 27; Metro Line, June 4, 1989; John A. Jones, "Metropolitan Financial Emerging as Midwest Powerhouse," Investor's Daily, October 19, 1989, p. 34; Ingrid Sundstrom and Joe Blade, "North Dakota Firm Buys Edina Realty," *Minneapolis Star and Tribune*, 1989, pp. 1A, 8A; Neal St. Anthony, "His Bread-and-Butter Style is Helping Thrift Firm Thrive," *Minneapolis Star and Tribune*, January 30, 1989, p.1D, 10D; Bill Nilles interview; interview of Steve DeWald, Fargo, March 15, 2007, hereafter DeWald interview; Tryhus interview; Annual Report, 1989.

2. Barth, pp. 97-98; Metro Hist., p.25-26; Annual Report, 1989, 1990; Steve Brook, "Metropolitan Moves On," *Saint Paul Pioneer Press,* December 23, 1990, pp.1-2 H; DeWald interview; Philip Matthews, "Metropolitan Moves Head Office," *The Forum*, September 28, 1990, p. B7, October 27, 1990; Tryhus interview; Norman Jones interview.

3. Clark interview; interview of Mark A. Jones, Fargo, July 11, 2007, hereafter Mark Jones interview; Gina A. Lauer, "Metropolitan Financial Services: Training Through Changes," *Bank Investment Representative*, November, 1994, pp.21, 22, 24, 52; Metro Hist. pp.27, 29, 31; Skurdall-Jones, p. 103; Annual Report 1991.

4. Norman M. Jones, Chairman and Lurence J. White, public member, "Savings Association Insurance Fund Industry Advisory Committee," July 2, 1992, pp. .3, 4, 5, 6, 8, 9, 11,14,15, 18, 20, 21, 23, 25, 26, hereafter SAIFIAC.

5. Jordahl interview; Clark interview; Bartkowski interview; Mike Nilles interview; Larsen interview; DeWald interview; Marcil interview; Dietz interview; Tryhus interview; Lee Schafer, "Error Apparent: Paul Lipetzky

Thought He Would Be Running Metropolitan Financial, Norman Jones Had Another Idea," *Corporate Report Minnesota*, pp. 52-55, 57, 59; Fedje interview; Eunice Jones interview.

6. Metro Hist., p..28; Neal St. Anthony, "Two Differ in Style, Approach," *Minneapolis Star and Tribune*, October, na, 1992, pp. D1, D6, D7; Martin J. Moylan, "On the Grow," *Saint Paul Pioneer Press*, November 23, 1992, pp. 1D, 3D; Tony Carideo, "Will National City Deal Bring Smiles All Around?," *Minneapolis Star and Tribune*, November 7, 1992, p.na; Skurdahl-Jones, p. 102; Dale Kurschner, "Metropolitan Financial May Buy Kansas Thrift," *The Business Journal*, pp. 1, 38; Annual Report, 1992; *The Forum*, October 28, 1992.

7. Tony Carideo, "At Metropolitan Financial, Latest Departure Raises Questions on Succession," *Minneapolis Star and Tribune*, June 22, 1993, p. 2D; Mary DeZutter, " Metropolitan Financial Chairman Considers Iowa, Nebraska Growth," *Omaha World Herald*, September 1, 1993, p. 18; Steve Klinkerman, "Metropolitan Financial to Buy a Wyoming Thrift," *American Banker*, September 28, 1993, p. 5; DeWald interview; Metro Hist., pp. 32-33; Annual Report, 1993.

8. Metro Hist. pp. 33, 36; Clark interview; Congratulatory letters in possession of the family; John Engen, "A Big Small-Town Acquirer: Exploiting Thrift Failures, Minnesota's Metropolitan Hit $7.8 Billion," *American Banker*, May 5, 1994, pp. 1 ,4-5; Bartkowski interview; Dewald interview; Tryhus interview; James P. Miller, "First Bank System Agrees to Purchase Metropolitan Financial for $863 Million," *The Wall Street Journal*, July 5, 1994, p. A6.

9. Letters from Paul T. Filipi, Omaha, August 11, 1994; Robert J Alyward, New York, July 9, 1994, in possession of the family; Seitz interview; Jonathan Knutson, "Going Out on Top: Metropolitan Federal Fades Into the Sunset Tuesday," *The Forum*, January 21, 1995, pp. B1, B3; Kellerman interview; Fedje interview; Metro Hist., p. 36; Jonathan Knutson, "Smile If You Bought Metropolitan Stock Early," *The Forum*, January 21, 1995, B-1; Jonathan Knutson, "A Glorious Run: Metropolitan Bank Exceeded Expectations," *The Forum*, February, 27, 1999, pp. B4, B10; Norm Jones interview.

10. Jonathan Knutson, "Going Out On Top: Metropolitan Federal Fades Into the Sunset Tuesday," *The Forum* January 21, 1995, pp. B1, B3; Norm Jones interview; Mark Jones interview; Jonathan Knutson, "A Glorious Run: Metropolitan Bank Exceeded Its Expectations," *The Forum*, February 27 1999, B4, B10; *The Forum*, October 10, 2000.

Chapter VII

A Three-Generation Legacy

B y now the reader probably has surmised that the Jones family was a devout, caring clan. This trait continued through each generation, which is most unusual. They set high standards for themselves and quietly expressed their faith by action.

Norm and Eunice Jones wanted this final chapter to express what they felt about values and obligation to society. In one respect their lives have focused on faith, family, and finances. In previous chapters I have indicated that those who were interviewed all reflected how pleased they were in their association with the family and Metropolitan.

Martin and Maurice Jones Sr.—Trendsetters

After nearly two decades of successful banking in Richland County, where he was well liked and had established an excellent reputation, Martin Jones and his family moved to Fargo where he continued his financial career. The family became involved with First Lutheran Church, and Martin began a nearly thirty-year association with the Fargo Union Mission, now the New Life Center, serving much of that time on the board. Birgit continued her activities with the ladies groups at First Lutheran.

Martin and Birgit's traits of strong family and religious values, as well as ethical business dealings, were passed on to their son, Maurice. In previous chapters many references were made to these qualities of Maurice. In 1995, twenty-four years after Maurice died, a friend and long-time business associate, David Rostad, wrote a letter to Kari Jones, Maurice's granddaughter, who was born several years after his death. The following quotes are from that letter.

"From 1962 until his death in 1971, I worked WITH him because he would not let you say FOR him. . . . [He believed] that every Metropolitan customer was the most important customer we had, whether that person had a $50 or a $100,000 account. They were all treated the same. He came out of his office many times a day to greet customers with a big smile and a handshake."

Rostad recalled that when he was setting up a partnership insurance agency with Metropolitan, the attorney who checked over the agreement said, "Mr. Rostad, Maurice Jones' word is worth more than any legal document you can have drawn up."

[Maurice's philosophy was that] there are three phases one goes through as an employee or as a member of an organization. The first is the dependent phase; the first day in a new situation one is nervous and wants to make a good impression. You realize that you are not very valuable, you try to learn fast but you probably are not earning your salary. You are dependent on others but you are trying to build your confidence. The second phase is when things improve and you have blossomed, and what did this outfit do before I came? I do more work than others but we get the same pay. You are in the me-me dependent phase. The what-have-they-done-for-me-lately attitude. The third phase is the happy marriage phase when employee and employer both realize that they have a good thing going—what is good for the company is good for me.

He taught us to look at the good side of things—he taught us positive thinking. The caring compassionate side. One of the staff came to Maurice and said they would like to fire one of the new tellers because she was "not working out." No one had ever been fired at Metropolitan up to that time, but when he was given all the details he said, "I don't like it, but I will accept your recommendation."

The next morning everyone was called into the coffee room and Maurice spoke. "Metropolitan suffered one of its first failures yesterday. We failed Beverly. Beverly didn't fail. We failed. We checked her references. We interviewed her. We agreed to hire her. We trained her. I feel very badly that we influenced her to accept us and now we rejected her. I hope

that we can learn from this unfortunate experience." . . .
I will never forget the expression of compassion by
Maurice. . . . He was a manager's manager like I have never
met before or since.

Maurice Jr. inherited the traits of his father. He was a real
people person. When he came to work at Metropolitan, he
realized that he was the newest employee and accepted it
with grace and quickly established a great relationship with
everyone. He maintained the respect of everyone after he
became president.

The Reverend Arthur W. Johnson, chaplain at St. Luke's
Hospital, said that even in his last days Maurice "listened with such
kindness and great fullness that one would set aside . . . [his or her]
own pity and cynicism and try to live up to his [Maurice's]
expectations of you. . . . One of Maurice Jones' fondest dreams was
to unite the spiritual and the physical in the life of the community.[1]

The Maurice Jones Memorial Lectureship
in Medicine and Religion

As part of his duties as chaplain, Johnson had attended a
number of noon medical lectures that caused him to wonder about
how physicians thought as diagnosticians and scientists. He
discussed the matter with his departmental colleague, Chaplain
Richard Einerson, and they concluded that there should be an
opportunity for the public to hear presenters who spoke on the
spiritual and ethical dimension of medicine. Johnson had served on
a Concordia committee that brought in outstanding speakers on the
topic, but they had not been heard by the general public. Einerson
proposed that they have lunch with his brother, David, who was a
vice president at Metro, and Norm. As a result of that meeting,
Metropolitan became the sponsor of an extended series of annual
lectures to be offered to the public on an evening in October along
with a morning and a noon presentation for medical residents at the
hospital or the clinic. The first free public presentations were meant
to be rotated among several community churches but eventually
were held at First Lutheran Church, the home congregation of the
Jones family.

The first lecture presented a new concept on the care of the dying at home, which was based on the theme of the hospice program. The second lecture focused on the care of leprosy patients. Other topics were about how a psychiatrist interfaced psychological and religious issues; worldwide eradication of smallpox; how a Christian looks at the death of a child, presented by Dr. Alvin Rogness, president of Luther Seminary who had lost a son. His opening thought set the tone for his address, "There are only two kinds of people in this world, people who believe in a benevolent, gracious God and those for whatever reason cannot." A real highlight was the presentation of a psychiatrist who had worked with many African Americans and had written six major studies on children's problems. He spoke about a six-year-old illiterate African American girl who was being forced to go to an integrated school. She stopped and bowed her head as she entered the school and prayed, "Father, forgive them for they know not what they do." The renowned Harvard psychiatrist said that that changed his life. The 1984 subject was mission medicine for women, which had a lasting impact on Chaplain Johnson: His daughter, Siri Fiebiger, was so struck by the topic that she went into medicine and then participated in medical mission trips. The final lecture in the series was moved to Moorhead State University because the pastor at First Lutheran would not permit it in the church. The topic was about the ethics of abortion by a professor of religion and a member of Catholic of Choice. All the lectures were attended by from 800 to 1,000 people and were highly acclaimed by those who participated.

During the twelve years that the above lectures were given, Morrie Jones fell victim to cancer and gave testimony about his diagnosis and bout with the disease. His presentation at First Lutheran was entitled "Coincidence or the Power of Prayer," which displayed his tremendous faith and his struggle during the previous five months.[2]

Church and Family

The first reference to any of Norm's participation in church was on May 13, 1945. The First Lutheran Church bulletin listed Norman Martin Jones as one of forty-three confirmands. Norm's name next appeared November 27, 1954, along with John H. Lunday Jr. when they headed a campaign to secure funds to purchase a new car for the pastor who was leaving the congregation after twenty-three years of service. "The promptness with which you act is quite as essential as the amount of your contribution. . . . We would rather have many small contributions than a few large ones. It is the fact that so *many* have given *something* which will mean the most to our good shepherd." Norm and Lunday were both in their early twenties and being selected to lead this project indicates that the leaders of First Lutheran, one of Fargo's largest churches, recognized them as do-ers. In November 1956 the pastor wrote Norm on another matter and added that he and his wife had taken a trip to the west coast and "the Pontiac carried us easily and comfortably. . . . I have been very thankful for that car down here [rural South Dakota] where I have to do lots of driving to do my pastoral work."

The March 8, 1974, Steeple Notes of the *Lutheran Standard* reported that Norman Jones was elected chairman of the district council. This was the first time that a lay person held the position which formerly had been chaired by the bishop of the district.

An article from the April 1964 *Readers' Digest* entitled "A Father Writes to His Son . . . . Don't Tell Me I've Got It Made" found in Norm's files gives insight to what guided him. The son had written to his father on his fifty-fifth birthday reminding him to relax because he had it made, to which the father replied,

> Dad could make all of this a lot less rough if he wanted to. Yes, I could; I could send you a check. But by doing so I would be robbing you of something. Life isn't having it made. Each necessary task requires an effort of will. And with each such act, something in you grows and is strengthened. . . . If you're ever unlucky enough to have it made, you will be a spectator, not a participant in life. You will look back wistfully from your security. . . . And you will know, too late, that it's the journey that counts, not the arrival.

Those who were close to Norm and Eunice knew that is how they lived during their working days.

In November 1990, after Norm was honored as Business Innovator of the Year, his eighty-three-year-old mother, Min, wrote, "I am proud of you. You are a very dedicated person. Thanks so much for you." She enclosed a note to Eunice, "This note wouldn't be complete unless I could thank you—your inspiration and help in every way has been and always will be such a big advantage to Norm. You're always ready with a smile and helping hand—his secretary too!"

On December 29, 2003, Norm's forty-one-year-old son, Steve, wrote:

A Tribute to My Dad. As a young man two of the most valuable things you gave me were a solid Christian foundation [through First Lutheran Church and our family devotion times] and a rich Norwegian heritage with all its wonderful traditions. . . . The legacy you have imparted to me is one of Christian love and complete sacrificial devotion to family and friends. It is my prayer and heartfelt desire that I will carry on this rich heritage that will also enrich and bless my own family and community.

Thirty-two-year-old Eric Jones, son of Nancy and the late Morrie Jones, wrote to Aunt Eunice and Uncle Norm after a visit with them.

You have been such a part of my life growing up. Eunice, Mom has talked so highly of you over the years. . . . Thanks for your servant example that embodies Christ. And thank you, Norm, for taking time for me and thinking of me. I think that it is amazing your focus has stayed so consistent. Not giving in to the trappings of the world. I have so much wanted to build a great company. It has consumed my thoughts since high school. But I have missed the point. I have missed the real goal. It doesn't seem to me that your goal or Morrie's was to become rich and famous, but to serve people and to love people. God is slowly teaching me to have my identity in Him and not in my work or successes. . . . I want to carry on this legacy of servant leadership.

Nancy Schafer told this writer twenty years after Morrie's death that Norm and Eunice "have always looked out for me and the children and still treat me like a sister. We will never know how many people those two have touched for Christ. They are such powerful examples of a Christ-centered living." After a visit to their lake cabin in the summer of 2006, Nancy wrote a thank you note:

"Thanks again for the many ways you continue to show your love for all of us. What a blessing you are to all who know you."[3]

Thoughts of Associates

David Piepkorn, a Fargo businessman and community leader, wrote to Norm, who he had known since childhood:

> The older I get, and the more people I come in contact with, the more I realize what an exceptional person you are. You have shown me what is truly important in life. Success has not changed your genuine beliefs and attitude. I have been blessed in so many ways in my life, and one of them is to have you as a role model. You have shown me how a Christian business leader should live, not just by what you say, but more importantly by what you do. . . . I have thought of these things for many years and I wanted to make sure you knew what a great example you are for me. Thank you.

Beverly Austin worked for Metropolitan for more than twenty-five years. In her later years she became senior vice president of MFB, the highest ranking female officer. She worked with Norm on a daily basis, and after Metro was sold, she wrote the following letter:

Dear Norman,

An exceptional company you have brought to being, nationally known and respected. I could never imagine that this opportunity could have happened to me. I thank you for the great growth personally that you allowed me. From the first day I met you, I could feel the exceptional abilities you possessed and the love and drive for the company. I am so proud to have known you and all you have stood for over these years. . . . Times have not always been easy; however, through everything you have stayed a person of great drive and love in what you set out to accomplish. . . . You are one-of-a-kind and this company past and present owes it to your leadership. It has been a wonderful time in my life and your love of the company has also been a love I have followed. I will miss that. However, I would not change my experiences for the world. Thank you.

To your continued success, signed, Beverly A. Austin.

A Hallmark card signed "All My Best to You, Judy" said: "I want to take this opportunity to let you know what a privilege it was to have worked for you at MFC. You are truly one-of-a-kind and will be a hard act to follow. I am pretty certain that [my new employer] won't bring me any latte coffee or share an occasional cookie. Only the most special people do things like that."

A senior vice president of MFC addressed his card,

Dear Mr. and Mrs. Jones, I would like to express my deepest gratitude to you for the profound honor of being able to work for Metropolitan Financial Corporation. The two of you have my highest esteem, respect, and admiration for the extraordinary Christian example you have given all of us as loving parents, devoted friends, and caring business owners. You will never realize how many lives are richer and more productive because you made people feel important and special. God's blessings, Tom Diffley.

Douglas Larsen, a board member since 1966, stated in an interview that he saw how Metro and the Jones family supported the community and many good causes. Watching them encouraged him to look at his business with a bigger picture and helped him expand his vision and become a better steward. The Joneses were real examples about how to live a meaningful life.[4]

Norm Takes Concordia's Fund-Raising To A New Level

Norm and Eunice have a warm spot in their hearts for Concordia College even though Norm spent only one and a half years there; Eunice had longed to go there but never had the opportunity. Both were well grounded in their faith, which to them included service to others and stewardship. First Lutheran was the first benefactor of their willingness to serve, but as soon as they had the means they turned to Concordia.

Linda Brown, who was assistant controller, added that in the 1970s the college was really desperate for a science hall, and raising the funds was the single biggest task it had experienced to that time.

The way Norm moved on the challenge was really bold. The cash donations were all meaningful, but more importantly, in 1973 Norm was elected to the board of regents where his leadership abilities played a key role in the decades ahead.

Everyone realized that Norm was a leader who was bold enough to move when he saw the way ahead. The science center was a far more costly building than any the college had built to that date. Paul Dovre, Concordia's president, knew that Norm was the person to head that campaign. Years later Dovre said,

> January 27, 1978, is a pivotal date in Concordia's history, for the college took the bold step of launching its first major fund drive. It needed increased annual support, a larger endowment fund, and a new biology and home economics facility and decided to raise $10.75 million in three years.

With the help of consultants, a campaign called Founders Fund I was created to complement the C-400 fund, which had been the only college fund-raising organization. C-400 had concentrated on small donors, and the consultants were very concerned because the college had no record of having big donors. They stressed that the college should not announce the campaign until most of the money was raised. Dovre recalled,

> Norm, who was an opportunist, built on his innate hopefulness plus his own imagination and energy that he brought to the campaign. We met every week in his office and each week we ground it out. Norm is the person who made it work. He would not take no for an answer. He put his creditability on the line and his optimism carried the ball. Norm was a source of encouragement all along—he simply was never in doubt about our ability to achieve our goal. He opened every meeting with prayer and kept foremost the spiritual dimension.

From conversations with Norm, Linda Brown, who attended all board meetings, said she learned that it was ingrained in both Norm and Eunice that giving is part of being a Christian.

On April 24, 1981, at the conclusion of the fund drive, Dovre announced that $12.05 million had been raised. Founders Fund I had surpassed its goal by almost $1.3 million, the most successful campaign in Concordia's history. Norm had taken fund-raising to a new level.

On December 9, 1982, Loren Anderson, Concordia's director of development, wrote to Norm alerting him that another campaign was being planned and, instead of relying so much on one person, a campaign cabinet, or steering committee, was being considered in which several people would be co-chairs. In addition to Norm, Bob Englestad, Norman Lorentzsen, J. Harry Johnson, Chester Reiten, Earl Olson, and Cliff Enger were asked to be on that committee. These individuals were well known in the Concordia community and were leading contributors.

Planning continued until January 13, 1984, when Dovre wrote to Norm, "You were part of the successful effort in Founders Fund I and we believe your commitment on behalf of Founders Fund II will be a bellwether again." The campaign was planned to stretch over four years with a goal of $21.5 million of which $14.5 million was designated for endowment and $7 million for operating expenses. Norm played a leading role in soliciting the business communities in Fargo-Moorhead and the Twin Cities where he was involved with fellowship groups of Christian businessmen. On April 6, 1986, it was announced that they surpassed their goal by raising $26.2 million. Linda Brown said, "It was clear that Norm was a real master of fund-raising." Fellow board member Gordon Eide commented that learning from Norm was like learning from the master.

After serving two terms on the board, he was off for a few years when Metro was expanding rapidly during the 1980s and then was called upon to serve two more terms. On November 23, 1988, Dovre called on the Joneses for more help. He wrote: "Norman and Eunice, you are 'leaders of the leaders' and have carried that mantle of Concordia for many years. Now again you carry that mantle in your commitment to the Centennial Fund." In late 1990 Norm stepped out of day-to-day management at Metro so he could spend more time on legislative issues and also devote more time to volunteer work. He served on the board of Lutheran Hospitals and Homes Society and also another Concordia campaign, which he co-chaired with Norman Lorentzsen, Ronald Offutt, and Loanne Thrane. On one occasion during the campaign

Norm was asked why Metro prospered when so many thrifts failed. He replied, "Honesty, integrity, and Christian values are as important in the corporate world as they are at a Christian college like Concordia. Some people think those values only belong in church on Sunday morning."

The Centennial Campaign, which was the third for Norm, lasted from 1989 to 1992 and had a goal of $46.5 million. By the end, $58.5 million was raised.

The Twenty-First Century Fund: Sustaining the Mission, which was Norm's final campaign, extended from 1995 to 2000. He co-chaired with Ronald Offutt. The campaign goal was $60 million; $71 million was raised.

Dovre spoke of his relationship with Norm as a regent:

Whenever I had a sensitive issue as president, Norm was a person I could go to because he could keep it to himself. He had the college at heart but he was not upset if the end decision did not go his way. He was a very good judge of people. He was a great help to us in picking people for the board and as fund-raisers. He had an incredible capacity for growth and the ability to see opportunities for growth. He helped the college with his farsighted investment strategies and paid attention to the basics but always kept his eyes open for opportunities, and he had the ability to think out of the box. He was bothered by some who were not good stewards. As a board member he was very good at working with people. He was very cooperative and irenic, a real team builder. I never saw any sign that he was ever under stress; he was that good at covering his feelings. Norman is comfortable in any group and can be one in the crowd. He does not have to push himself forward, and neither he nor Eunice seek the spotlight. Eunice is such a strong partner and Norm freely admitted her influence.

The administration of Concordia had long realized that Norm and Eunice had made an exceptional contribution in time, talent, and treasure and wanted to do something to commemorate their efforts. The opportunity came October 4, 1998, when the Jones Science Center was dedicated in their honor. President Dovre told the audience:

Norm and Eunice in front of the Jones Science Center at Concordia College, October 4, 1998.

Founders Fund I was organized, and we realized that it needed dedicated people like Norman and Eunice Jones to head the national campaign. Norman and Eunice were dedicated and faithful servants with a passion to serve, and they led by example with generously sharing their time and treasure. Norman and Eunice have played an important part helping the college attain a new level of development in its pursuit of excellence. Eunice, who volunteers for many other activities, holds family, church, and community as her key interests in life and in their philanthropic mission. It is not possible to describe adequately the powerful and strategic role Norm and Eunice Jones have played in the development of the college over the past twenty years. They have always been in the vanguard and what they said with their lips they expressed in their deeds. When the story of this quarter century in the chronicle of the college's history is told, their names will be "writ large."

Then, as a postscript to his message, Dovre quoted II Corinthians 3:5, "For there is nothing in us that allows us to claim we are capable of doing this work. The capacity we have comes from God; for it is he who makes us capable of serving the new covenant."

Norm and Eunice both gave responses to Dovre's commendation address. After Norm had given his response, Eunice voiced her feelings. She started her response by saying she was reminded of the story of the mouse and the elephant crossing the bridge. After they got across, the mouse said to the elephant, "We sure made that bridge shake."

In addition to having a building named in their honor, in 1991 Norm received the Centennial Medallion, which was given to only eleven individuals "whose lives have embodied the mission of the college." In 1994 he received the Concordia Alumni Achievement Award, and on May 2, 1999, he was awarded an honorary doctorate. The citation noted that he had served four terms on the Concordia board of regents. This put him in a very unique crowd. During his first three terms he always declined to serve as chair, but Dovre added that he made up for that as a fund-raiser and served very well as an advisor. However, in his fourth term he agreed to serve as chairman.[5]

Luther Seminary's First Major Gift

Dr. David Tiede, president of Luther Seminary, first met Norm Jones on a trip to Moorhead in 1989 specifically for the purpose of meeting him and later to ask him to serve on the seminary board. He had heard many good things about Norm and had a positive first impression "but I did not realize what a marvelous idea it was nor did I realize what a marvelous human being he is." Tiede commented that after the entire committee was formed to conduct a major fund drive, they were assembled and each one was asked to give testimony as to why they volunteered to serve.

> A few days after that meeting, Norm called and asked if he could see the campus. I was amazed at how attentive he was. He was always asking key questions and had no time for minutiae. Later my wife and I met with Eunice and found another just like Norm. I then saw how strong their convictions were and how their personal goals came together. The next time we met Norm had the solutions and I knew what to do. That was the routine from then on. I would tell him my problem, and the next time we met he knew the answer and I could go from there. If I had to sum up my convictions in one statement it would be that Norman and Eunice are people of Christian wisdom.

Tiede then injected, "You don't want to take Eunice lightly; she is so deep and strong. She has never forgotten her very modest beginnings. Norman likes to quote Norman Lorentzsen, who always challenges, with one comment, 'One thing I can promise you, if you make this big gift you will never regret it.' Then he comments about feeling happy about giving."

Tiede said Norm got him to join a Bible study group. Norm was conscious of Tiede having a PhD while he had only a year and a half of college. "He would say to me, 'Now don't spoil how we do it. We know you are a professor of New Testament but we don't want you to spoil how we are discussing it [the Bible lesson].'" Tiede mentioned that he had felt lonesome on the top as president of the seminary and he imagined how Norm must have felt at Metro.

> Being with Norman was so relaxing because he was like an older brother. Norm and Eunice didn't really know about the seminary but they wanted the Lutheran Church to be a witness to the Gospel. They gave me a new perspective about how I should lead at the seminary. All I had to know was, what would it do for the Gospel of Christ? Norm was the spiritual leader of the Foundation because of his clear sense of the Gospel. He knows that to raise money you have to have your house in order to get the job done. He has the practical wisdom with a Christ-centered heart.

The Second Half of Our Lives

During the early 1990s Norm and Eunice attended a conference on what to do with the second half of your life. Linda Brown, who was then director of development at Concordia and had worked with Norm and Eunice, commented that the conference was a turning point that cemented their decision about fund-raising, gifting, and working with people who were interested in philanthropy. Ronald Offutt and Norm made calls on people who were "heavyweights with Concordia interests" and enjoyed the experience. Offutt concurred with Norm's basic outlook on philanthropy and the mission of the church and added, "This is what led Norm and Eunice to be the first big contributors to Luther Seminary." Norm and Eunice were particularly interested in the seminary because its alumni mostly worked in the church and did not have the potential to be big donors. Prior to the merger in 1992, most of the scholarship money had come from the national church, but that was discontinued.

The fall/winter 1993 issue of *The Luther Northwestern Story* contained the following article: "Hatlen, Jones Families Announce One Million Dollar Matching Gift." President Tiede made the surprise announcement that the two families had "agreed to make this unprecedented challenge gift to urge each of you, as well as thousands of other friends and alums, to increase their support of the seminary's sustaining fund." Norm gave a response:

> Fund-raising needs four basic ingredients: a good staff, lots of volunteers, people willing to give of their talents and their money, and a great cause. . . . What better cause is there than to train men and women to send them out to the world to proclaim the Gospel of Jesus Christ?

Norm continued, "The seminary is Bible centered, and most important it is Christ centered. . . . Without Jesus Christ there is nothing. That is why we . . . Eunice and I, are more than pleased to be part of this program."

On May 23, 1997, the same periodical carried an article entitled "Norman and Eunice Jones Have a Calling," in which Norman commented, "We know our calling is to preach the Gospel. Some can do it personally by being pastors and missionaries, and some can support those who do. We thought we could use our talent to raise money in support of theological education." Eunice was quoted: "It is exciting to see the fruits of our giving. . . . Both of our families were centered in the Christian life. Giving and serving seemed very natural. That was where the heart was. Though my family was poor when I was growing up on the farm, we were tithers."

David and Martha Tiede summed up what Norm and Eunice meant to the cause:

> You accepted our call when we needed it most. You have listened, counseled, and cared for us and the seminary. You helped us design the Perfect Match challenge, stepped up to

the challenge, and brought many others with you in your witness. . . . We thank God for you.[6]

Much of the activity discussed in this chapter took place while Norm was still leading Metropolitan. In 1995, after forty-three years of giving 110 percent effort and after the sale of Metropolitan, Norm and Eunice experienced a rapid change in lifestyle. They moved back to Fargo where they felt they could have the greatest impact for the second half of their lives. They were blessed with talents that few people possess. This gave them the wherewithal necessary to be such a bountiful blessing to society.

~ ~ ~ ~ ~

1. David Rostad letter of Tribute to Maurice H. Jones Sr., written to Kari Jones, September 29, 1995, in files; *Binford Guide*, December 1978.
2. A typed summary of the Lectureship series from Rev. Arthur W. Johnson, May 10, 2008, Richville, Minnesota; *Metro Line* October 1984, September 1985, September 1986, March 1989; *The Forum* November 3, 1985.
3. First Lutheran Church bulletin, May 13, 1945; Norm Jones and John Lunday letter November 27, 1954, to members of the First Lutheran congregation; letter from Rev. Selmer A. Berge, Elk Point, South Dakota, November 29, 1956, to Norman Jones; *Lutheran Standard*, March 8, 1974; *Readers' Digest*, April 1964, pp.90-92; Min Jones, Thank You Note, November 4, 1990, to Norm and Eunice Jones; letter from David Piepkorn, Fargo, September 2000, to Norm Jones; letter from Steven Jones, December 29, 2003, to Norm Jones; Eric Jones letter July 2007, to Norm and Eunice Jones; Schafer interview; Nancy Schafer undated letter to Norm and Eunice Jones.
4. Letter from Beverly A. Austin, January 9, 1995; an undated card from Terry (Clark) Pederson; an undated card signed Judy; an undated card from Tom Diffley; Larsen interview.
5. Concordia College minutes and records for board members and development programs; interview of Paul J. Dovre, President emeritus, Concordia College, Moorhead, Minnesota, April 17, 2007, hereafter Dovre interview; interview of Linda Brown, Vice President for Development, Concordia College, Moorhead, Minnesota, April 10, 2007, hereafter Brown interview.
6. Interview of David L. Tiede, Roseville, Minnesota, May 31, 2007; interview of Ronald Offutt, Fargo, April 19, 2007; Brown interview; *The Luther Northwestern Story*, Fall/Winter, 1993, pp.8-10, May 23, 1997; letter from David and Martha Tiede, Roseville, Minnesota, July 13, 1994.

Bibliography

Public Documents

Annual Reports of the Building and Loan Associations of the State of North Dakota. Bismarck: 1930-1952.

Annual Report of the Federal Home Loan Bank of Des Moines. April 23, 1952.

Cass County ND Court Proceedings. February 16, 1925-September 3, 1931.

North Dakota State Banking Board Report. July 1, 1920-June 30, 1922.

Report of Norman Jones, Chairman, Savings Association Insurance Fund Industry Advisory Committee, on "The Adequacy of the Savings Association Insurance Fund. July 2, 1992.

Richland County, ND, *Book of Original Entries*. July 16, 1897-October 4, 1922.

Bulletins, Newspapers, Periodicals

Binford, Howard. "Maurice H. Jones, One of Metropolitan's Founders in 1926," *Howard Binford's Guide*, Vol. 11, No .6, December 1978, pp 24, 44.

Breckenridge (Minn.) *Telegram*. January 12, 1895.

The DeLamere (ND) *Mistletoe*. January 22, 1914-May 22, 1919.

The Fargo (ND) *Forum*, also *The Forum*. 1926-2005.

Grand Forks Herald. 1968- 1995.

Investor's Daily. October 19, 1989.

Klinkerman, Steve. "Metropolitan Financial to Buy a Wyoming Thrift," *American Banker*. September 28, 1993.

Kurschner, Dale. "Metropolitan Financial May Buy Kansas Thrift," *Money Business, The Business Journal*, November 13-19, 1992.

Lauer, Gina A. "Metropolitan Financial Services: Thriving Through Change," *Bank Investment Representative: The Magazine of Investment Marketing and Investment Program Management*, Vol. 4 #11, November 1994.

The Lisbon (ND) *Free Press*. July 27, 1905-1918.

The Minneapolis Star-Tribune. 1987-1995.

Minot (ND) *Daily News*. June 22, 1974.

Omaha World Herald. September 1, 1993.

Richland County (ND) *Gazette.* July 21, 1899.

Saint Paul Pioneer Press. 1987-1995.

Sargent County (ND) *Teller.* June 27, 1906-1916.

Schafer, Lee. "Error Apparent: Paul Lipetzky Thought He Would be Running Metropolitan Financial, Norman Jones Had Another Idea," *Corporate Report Minnesota.* December 1992.

Valley City (ND) *Times Record.* November 19, 1974.

The Wahpeton (ND) *Gazette.* July 24, 1903.

The Wall Street Journal. July 5, 1994.

The Wyndmere (ND) *Enterprise.* October 5, 1907-1914.

The Wyndmere (ND) *Pioneer.* January 21, 1916-May 10, 1918.

Books

Barth, James R. *The Great Savings and Loan Debacle.* Washington, D.C.: The American Enterprise Institute, 1991.

Carron, Andrew S. *Studies in the Regulation of Economic Activity.* The Plight of the Thrift Institutions." Washington, D.C.: The Brookings Institution, 1982.

Carron, Andrew S. "The Rescue of the Thrift Industry." Washington, D.C.: The Brookings Institution, 1983.

Crawford, Lewis F. *History of North Dakota.* Chicago: American Historical Society, 1931.

Danbom, David B. *Going It Alone: Fargo Grapples With the Great Depression.* St. Paul: Minnesota Historical Society Press, 2005.

Ewalt, Josephine Hedges. *A Business Reborn: The Savings and Loan Story, 1930-1960.* Chicago: American Savings and Loan Institute Press, 1962.

Metropolitan Financial Corporation 1926-1995. Privately printed, 1995.

Pressly, Thomas J, and William H. Scofield. *Farm Real Estate Values in the United States by Counties 1850-1959.* Seattle: University of Washington Press, 1965.

Robinson, Elwyn B. *History of North Dakota.* Lincoln: University of Nebraska Press, 1966.

Skurdall, James. *A Berg Family History: Gol, Hollingdal to Richland County, North Dakota.* Privately printed, 2003.

Skurdall, James. *Henry and Mary Ann Immigrants from Sogn: The Jones Family in America 1857-2001.* Privately printed, 2001.

Wrigley, Edmund. *The Working Man's Way to Wealth: A Practical Treatise on Building Associations: What They Are and How to Use Them.* Philadelphia: James K. Simon, 1872.

Wyndmere Centennial 1985.

Unpublished Material

Annual Reports of Metropolitan, 1983-1993.

Austin, Beverly A. Letter, January 9, 1995, to Norman Jones, in Jones file.

Aylward, Robert J. Letter, August 11, 1994, to Norman Jones, in Jones file.

Berge, Selmer A. Letter, November 29, 1956, to Norman Jones, in Jones file.

Concordia College, Citations, correspondence, minutes and publications of matters with Eunice and Norman Jones, at the college or in Jones file.

Dahl, Howard. Manuscript of a Eulogy of Morrie Jones, December 15, 1987, in Nancy Schafer file.

Davis, James A. An E-mail, regarding North Dakota banking regulations in the 1920s.

Gate City Savings and Loan, Minutes, March 18, 1925-March 25, 1926.

Grube, Nanette. Letter, January 8, 2004, to Norman Jones, in Jones file.

Hanson, Kathy. Letters, September 26, 1996, December 28, 2005, to Norman Jones, in Jones file.

Johnson, Arthur W. A Resume of the Maurice Jones Lectureship Series, in possession of this writer.

Jones, Maurice H. "A History of Metropolitan Savings and Loan," an undated typed manuscript c.a. 1965.

Jones, Min. Undated letter to Eunice and Norman Jones, in Jones file.

Jones, Norman M. and John H. Lunday Jr. Letter November 27, 1954, to members of First Lutheran Church, in Jones file.

Jones, Steve. Letter, December 29, 2003, to Norman Jones, in Jones file.

Luther Seminary, Citations, correspondence, and publications regarding relations with Eunice and Norman Jones, in Jones file.

MetroLine, an in-house newsletter published March 1974-December 1989.

Metropolitan brochure, September 24, 1955, in memory of Martin Jones and for the dedication of the new building.

Metropolitan Financial Corporation 1926-1995. A company history, 1995.

Offering Circular, i.e. Prospectus, March 24, 1983.

Olson, Ole A. "The Martin and Birgit Jones Family: Tributes, Reminiscences, and Reflections." A typed manuscript, dated 1954, in Jones file.

Piepkorn, David. Letter September 2000 to Norman Jones, in Jones file.

Rostad, David. Letter, September 29, 1995, to Kari Jones, in Nancy Schafer file.

Scrapbook on Going Public, in possession of Norman Jones.

Tiede, David and Martha. Letter July 13, 1994, to Eunice and Norman Jones, in Jones file.

Tryhus, Trueman. Letter November 11, 1987, to Morrie Jones, in Nancy Schafer file.

Interviews

Anderson, Marlys Powers. Fargo, August 13, 2007.

Bartkowski, William P. Minnetonka, May 31, 2007.

Bladow, Clarence. Richville, May 8, 2008.

Brown, Linda. Moorhead, April 10, 2007.

Clark, Bob. Fargo, April 25, 2007, and several conversations.

DeWald, Steve. Fargo, March 15, 2007.

Dietz, Gary. Fargo, March 13, 2007, and several conversations.

Dovre, Paul J. Moorhead, April 17, 2007, and several conversations.

Fedje, Noel. Fargo, May 9, June 13, 2007.

Golberg, Allen. Lake Park, June 27, 2007.

Green, David. Lake Park, June 27, 2007.

Hartman, Linette. Moorhead, March 13, 2007.

Holt, Benjamin. Fargo, May 4, 1977.

Horn, Joan. Fargo, March 20, 2007.

Ihry, Betty. Pelican Rapids, March 19, 2007.

Jones, Eunice M. Fargo, A series of interviews in April and May 2007 and ongoing conversations.

Jones, Mark A. Fargo, July 11, 2007.

Jones, Norman M. Fargo, A series of interviews in April and May 2007 and

ongoing conversations.

Jordahl, Rodney. Fargo, March 21, 2007.

Kellerman, Dorothy Borderud. Fargo, May 24, 2007.

Kvamme, Richard. Moorhead, April 11, 2007.

Larsen, R. Douglas. Fargo, May 21, 2007, and several conversations.

Lysne, David. Fargo, April 30, 2007.

Marcil, William C. Sr. Fargo, May 15, 2007.

Nilles, Michael (Mike). Eden Prairie, May 31, 2007.

Nilles, William (Bill). Lake Park, March 19, 2007.

Offutt, Ronald D. Fargo, April 19, 2007.

Renner, Anthony (Tony). Moorhead, May 7, 2007, and several conversations.

Schafer, Nancy Jones. Fargo, May 8, 2007.

Sweet-Seitz, Eilene. Fargo, April 23, 2007, and several conversations.

Tiede, David L. Roseville, May 31, 2007.

Tryhus, Trueman. Fargo, May 19, 2007.

Vandrovec, Bev Thompson. Fargo, March 20, 2007.

Index